Co-stars of the Acts of the Apostles

— PATRICK WHITWORTH —

Sacristy
Press

Sacristy Press
PO Box 612, Durham, DH1 9HT

www.sacristy.co.uk

First published in 2025 by Sacristy Press, Durham

Sacristy Limited, registered in England
& Wales, number 7565667

British Library Cataloguing-in-Publication Data
A catalogue record for the book is
available from the British Library

ISBN 978-1-78959-376-1

Contents

Foreword

We often read the Acts of the Apostles as the story of the church in Jerusalem and Paul's missionary journeys. It is easy for us to feel it is about Apostle Peter's amazing preaching and Apostle Paul's travelling to the ends of the earth. But as Patrick reminds us, there is also a whole team of co-stars serving one another as prophets, evangelists, pastors and teachers who enabled the apostles to do their mighty acts. In the same way Paul teaches us about the concept of the body of Christ, Luke likewise records for us who had which ministries and how the Holy Spirit orchestrates the body according to God's plan.

Jesus modelled choosing 12 apprentices and Paul followed this pattern by training and releasing Timothy, Silas and Titus. This is how many ministers lead their churches today, encouraging members to serve the community, to lead home groups, to lead services and to try preaching a sermon. Again and again God has generously poured out his grace and as in the Acts of the Apostles many are still being called into full-time ministry.

I recommend Patrick's book as the basis of a sermon and home group series "The co-stars of the Acts". I hope and pray this book will inspire both church leaders to encourage and release others, and church members to see that in the past ordinary, everyday followers of Jesus have shaped the church, and there is every hope that they will do so again!

Michael Saunders
Vicar of St Lawrence, Hungerford

Preface

In his epistles, the Apostle Paul often speaks about the church being the body of Christ. It is probably his favourite metaphor for describing the church, as it combines both the dynamic of unity, together with the truth of diversity (see 1 Corinthians 12; Romans 12:3–8; Ephesians 4:1–13). But it is Luke who shows how this concept works out in practice, and he does this especially in his second great narrative, the Acts of the Apostles which records the spread of the church through the Roman Empire (see Luke 1:3; Acts 1:1).

This present, short book is designed as an introduction to the idea that in the Acts of the Apostles there are a number of people with differing gifts who equipped the church both to build up its own community and to reach out to the society of the first century. I have called them *co-stars,* picking up Paul's phrase written to the Philippians that those who follow the way of Christ will be like stars shining in the heavens (Philippians 2:15b). They were certainly vital in the corporate mission of the church in this period and examples of the diversity of gifting granted to the body of Christ by the Spirit.

Although the two central characters in the Acts are Peter and Paul, both relied on others to develop and demonstrate God's love for the world.

This book brings together this group of *co-stars* or co-workers in such a way as to show how much the body of Christ was and is dependent on the contribution of the many for its own life and mission.

Often the chief focus is on the main leader, a Peter or a Paul, and with justification, but without these others they would quickly become ineffective and isolated.

What we will notice as we go through Acts is the rich diversity of people, characters and background of those who spearhead the mission of God to the world. All are needed. To use Paul's own metaphor of the body of Christ: "If we were all heads, where would the body be? If we were all toes, where would the strategic thinking be? Or if we were all mouth, where would the listening be?" (1 Corinthians 12). Indeed, all are needed. And through this range of men and women, Jew and Greek, slave and free, the church was able to reach out to the whole community. So, let's celebrate this rich variety of disciples with their own specific gifts and roles and be amazed at what Paul calls this multi-layered and multi-coloured rainbow-grace of God (see Ephesians 3:10).

Once again, I would like to thank Dr Natalie Watson of Sacristy Press, and Mike Saunders for his kind Foreword and, more importantly, for exhibiting the principles behind this book in his own church, St

Lawrence's Hungerford. Finally, but not least, thanks to Olivia, my wife of 45 years.

Patrick Whitworth
29 June 2024
The Feast of St Peter and St Paul
who relied on these co-stars

The encourager: Barnabas

Acts 4:36–37; 9:26–29; 11:25–30; 13:1–3; 15:36–41

By the time Barnabas emerged at the forefront of the church's expansion in Jerusalem and Judea, the church was still barely a few months old. The church—or the community of believers who were the church by virtue of being the "called out ones" or the *ekklesia*—had been formed on the basis of the significant acts recorded at the end of Luke's Gospel and at the beginning of the book of Acts. These acts were the death and resurrection of Jesus (Luke 23 and 24), the ascension of Jesus (Acts 1:10,11), and the gift of the Spirit at Pentecost (Acts 2). These events defined and constituted the new community, the members of which, later in Acts, came to be called Christians (see Acts 11:26b). Interestingly, they were first called Christians in the much more mixed setting of Jews and Gentiles in the imperial regional centre of the east at Antioch.

The church was first formed by the gift of the Spirit, which came after the exaltation of Jesus (Acts 2:24,33) and his atoning death (Acts 2:23). This is made clear by the Apostle Peter in his great address on the Day of Pentecost (Acts 2). All those who believed in Jesus were to be included in the new community through their repentance and faith, their baptism in the name of Jesus Christ, and their consequent reception of the Holy Spirit (2:38). Once included in this community of salvation, they formed part of the church, which had its own leadership, the apostles, and also its own pattern of life centred around the teaching of the apostles, the fellowship, the breaking of bread, and the prayers (see Acts 2:42–47). This quadrilateral of spiritual discipline formed the basic life of this community, and, at some point soon after the beginning of the church at Pentecost, Barnabas must have joined, becoming a devoted follower of Jesus Christ and member of the church.

Before looking at Barnabas's particular contribution to the church, it is worth sketching in the nature of the Christian community in Jerusalem. The German New Testament scholar Joachim Jeremias estimated the regular population of Jerusalem in the time of Jesus was approximately 25–30,000, although more recent scholarship has the settled population at about 60,000.[1]

---

[1] James D. G. Dunn, *Beginning from Jerusalem, Vol. II of Christianity in the Making* (Grand Rapids, MI: Wm. B. Eerdmans, 2009), p. 176, fn. 24.

However, at the times of the main Jewish festivals, the population could rise to as many as 200,000. Of this settled population, as many as 50,000 were involved in the specific religious communities of Judaism as either priests, Levites, pharisees or scribes, and their families. On the Day of Pentecost, the numbers in Jerusalem were probably running into the hundreds of thousands, all crammed into the relatively small city which was bounded by walls and included the Temple Mount.

Luke tells us the festival population of Jerusalem included Jews from Parthia, Medes, Elamites, residents of Mesopotamia, Judea, Cappadocia, Pontus, Asia, and Phrygia, as well as those from North Africa, including Libya and Egypt, and from islands like Cyprus and Crete (see Acts 2:8–12). Luke also tells us that on the Day of Pentecost about 3,000 were added to the church in a single day (2:41). Many, it seems, were from the pilgrim population attending the festival, and they heard the apostles telling the wonders of God in their own tongues (Acts 2:6,11).

Barnabas

We know little of the back story of Barnabas, except that he was from Cyprus, that his real name was Joseph, and that he was soon known by the apostles as Barnabas, meaning "Son of Encouragement". Barnabas most likely came from the eastern end of the island of Cyprus, closest to Palestine and Syria and from the classical city of Salamis. Barnabas (or Joseph) was a Levite, which means that he was a member of the tribe appointed by Moses to assist the priests in the ceremonies of the Tabernacle and then of the Temple (see Numbers 18 and Deuteronomy 18). He was, as we shall see, a property holder in both Cyprus and Jerusalem. It seems that Barnabas had become part of the Jewish *diaspora* living permanently in Cyprus but had come to Jerusalem for the festival of Pentecost where he became a follower of Jesus, the Messiah or Christ.

A generous giver

It is clear that Barnabas was a generous man. He may have already been a generous man even before he became a follower of Jesus, but now, as a follower of Jesus, he became even more so.

Generosity lies at the heart of our faith. It is clear from the prologue of John's Gospel that generosity was a chief characteristic and quality of Jesus's incarnate life. John expresses this by saying, "From the fullness of his grace we have all received one blessing after another [or grace upon grace]" (1:16). Jesus demonstrated this generosity in his first miracle in Cana of Galilee, where he made some 600 litres of the highest quality wine for a wedding party that was running out of wine altogether (see John 2:1–11). Likewise, in famous verses in the midst of his teaching about giving to the Corinthians, Paul writes memorably: "For you know the grace of our Lord Jesus Christ, that though he was rich yet for your sake he became poor, so that you through his poverty might become rich" (2 Corinthians 8:9). Generosity was therefore intrinsic to the whole coming of Christ, that he became poor that we might become rich, and was a quality born in Jesus's followers.

Generosity can take many forms: generosity with our time to others, and generosity in our appraisal of others, but most frequently it can mean generosity with our resources. There is little doubt that Barnabas would have found the way of life of the early church in Jerusalem inspiring. We are told: "All the believers were together and had everything in common. Selling their possessions and goods, they gave to anyone who had need" (Acts 2:44,45). This practice is elaborated two chapters later, where Luke tells us again: "There were no needy persons among them. From time to time those who owned lands or houses sold them, brought the money from the sales, and put it at the apostles' feet, and it was distributed to anyone who had need" (Acts 4:34,35). Barnabas followed suit. He "sold a field he owned and brought the money and put it at the apostles' feet" (Acts 4:37). No doubt Barnabas experienced the truth that "God is able to make all grace abound to you, so that in all things, at all times having all that you need, you will abound in every good work" (2 Corinthians 9:8). In line with his generous nature, it seems that Barnabas was also generous in his speech and expressions, and instead of being called Joseph, gained the nickname Barnabas, which means "Son of Encouragement".

The encourager

Some years ago, I took part in a mission in Fort Portal, Uganda, among the Rutooro-speaking people of the Rwenzori region. We were a team of six and after about three days, when they had come to know us, we were each given a nickname. I think mine was Abwale, which means something like teacher, and which seemed quite fitting. It is clear from the Bible that Jesus often gave people pet names or nicknames: James and John were called "Sons of Thunder" and Simon was called Peter, meaning rock, and no doubt there were others too. It seems that Joseph was quickly given the nickname Barnabas by the apostles because of his encouraging nature. The transliteration of the Hebrew name Barnabas in Greek is *uíós paraklésiōs* or "Son of Encouragement", and as a matter of interest the word for encouragement is the same name given by John to the Holy Spirit, "paraclete", the one who draws alongside to help (John 14:26). Like the Spirit, Barnabas was one who "draws alongside to help". It seems that this is exactly what he did. It was Barnabas who provided the link between the Apostle Paul and the church and the apostles in Jerusalem, and it was Barnabas who provided encouragement to the church at Antioch.

In both instances Barnabas was a bridge builder. When Paul was converted on the Damascus Road, there was much suspicion about the genuineness of his conversion. Could one who had been so vehement in his persecution of the church so radically and suddenly change? Thus, when he came to Jerusalem after his conversion, the disciples "were all afraid of him, not believing that he really was a disciple" (Acts 9:26; Galatians 1:17,18). But Barnabas stood up for Paul as his "advocate", telling the disciples that the Lord had spoken to him, and that Paul had "preached fearlessly in the name of Jesus" in Damascus before having to flee. In this way, Barnabas allayed the fears of the Christian community in Jerusalem and helped them forge a vital bond with Paul for the future of Christianity. Being a bridge builder is important for bringing people together and harnessing the gifts of all for the good of the church.

Not only did Barnabas introduce Paul to the church in Jerusalem and reassure them, but with great discernment he also forged a bond between Paul and the most missionary-minded church of the time at Antioch. The background to the church at Antioch was that converts from Cyprus and from Cyrene (Libya) had gone outside the Jewish community to evangelize the Greek community there, with the result that many Antiochenes had turned to the Lord. When news of this move of God came to the ears of the leaders in Jerusalem, they decided to check it out and so sent Barnabas as their envoy. What he found was a thriving church. He urged them "to remain true to the Lord with all their hearts", encouraging and affirming them. At the same time, he realized that if they were to reach their full potential, they needed a more gifted teacher than he. Not only was Barnabas an encourager, but he realized the limitations of his own gifts, and prepared the way for others more gifted than himself to take the limelight. And so, he went to Tarsus to find Paul.

Paul had gone to Tarsus from Jerusalem in AD 36 when it was no longer safe to remain in Jerusalem (Acts 9:29,30). He would remain in Tarsus until AD 46.[2] What we do not often grasp is the sheer length of time Paul spent in preparation for his world-changing ministry in what we might consider was the backwater of Tarsus—ten years. Barnabas evidently persuaded Paul to go with him. By then, Paul must have been wondering how he was going to fulfil the words spoken to Ananias (and presumably shared with Paul) that he was a chosen instrument of God, intended to "carry my name before the Gentiles and their kings and before the people of Israel" (Acts 9:15). The pair returned to Antioch together, to probably the largest church in the Near East at the time, and for a whole year they met with the church and taught great numbers of people.

---

[2]   This chronology is taken from Tom Wright's timeline in *Paul: A Biography* (London: SPCK, 2020), p. 433.

Humanly speaking, this ministry came about through the discernment, humility and inclusive contacts of Barnabas. Where others might have been afraid of the persecutor-of-the-church-turned-apostle, Barnabas gave Paul the right hand of welcome. Where others might have sought fame for themselves by teaching the largest church in Christendom, Barnabas knew that someone with greater gifts than his own was needed. And where another might have resented the greater role given to Paul as an apostle, Barnabas recognized that this was the will of God. But their time together in the relative calm of Antioch was short-lived. The Holy Spirit was about to move them on with the words heard during worship: "Set apart for me Barnabas and Saul for the work to which I have called them" (Acts 13:2).

The missionary

This first missionary journey, recorded in Acts 13–15, was a breathless expedition to Cyprus and then into the interior of Pisidia. Understandably they first went to Cyprus, Barnabas's home island, and to its two principal cities, Salamis and Paphos. Both were important Greek and then Roman colonies, but in Paphos the opportunity arose to speak to the proconsul, Sergius Paulus, in the context of a powerful sign of judgement (Acts 13:9–11). The proconsul believed, and Saul took his name, Paul.

It appears from the account of the remainder of the missionary journey that Paul and Barnabas had distinct roles. Not unexpectedly, given his great learning and background, Paul took the lead when it came to preaching and teaching. After all, it was because of that gifting that Barnabas had brought Paul to Antioch from Tarsus in the first place. In Lystra, the population, inordinately impressed by the healing of a lame man, thought that Barnabas and Paul were gods. "Barnabas they called Zeus and Paul they called Hermes because he was the chief speaker" (Acts 14:12). I imagine they settled into these roles. Presumably Barnabas had the physical stature to be called Zeus, while Paul was the one who grasped the podium, or who spoke first in the synagogues. Paul's synagogue address in Pisidian Antioch is a classic of its kind, giving us true insight into the content of Paul's teaching to the Jews about Jesus. The main thrust of his argument is summarized by the words, "We tell you the good news: What God promised our ancestors he has fulfilled for us, their children, by raising up Jesus. . . . Therefore, my friends, I want you to know that through Jesus the forgiveness of sins is proclaimed to you. Through him everyone who believes is set free from every sin, a justification you were not able to obtain under the law of Moses" (Acts 13:32,33,38,39). Here too are the seeds of Paul's later letter to the Galatians, who were in severe danger of going back on the good news they had heard (see Galatians 3:11–14). It was doubtless an argument and declaration that Barnabas was familiar with, and that he preached himself (Acts 14:3).

The mission to the cities of Pisidia, which included Pisidian Antioch, Iconium (present-day Konya), Lystra, and Derbe, was successful. "A great number of Jews and Gentiles believed" (Acts 14:1). Many miraculous signs were given. Much opposition was also stirred up (Acts 14:3–5). For Barnabas it must have been an extraordinary experience and one that marked him for life. But it was also to reveal Barnabas's deep attachment to another member of the party, and the trouble this caused him.

The loyal companion

We have already seen that Barnabas was very much a people person. It was he (ironically, as we shall see) who recognized the authenticity of Paul's conversion and introduced him to the apostles and the church in Jerusalem when they were frankly frightened of Paul and were questioning the validity of his conversion. It was Barnabas who saw Paul's ability to instruct and prepare the church in Antioch and who brought him from Tarsus for the task. Quite clearly Barnabas appreciated and esteemed the potential of others, preferring their interests to his own (see Philippians 2:4). He was committed to Paul, recognizing his God-given calling, but he was also committed to John Mark, who had accompanied them on this missionary journey and who was quite probably a relative of Barnabas.

John or John Mark, later the writer of Mark's Gospel, was a close associate of Peter in Rome.[3] Luke tells us that John Mark had earlier accompanied Paul and Barnabas on a visit to Jerusalem from Antioch (12:25) and that he also went with them on the mission to Cyprus (13:4–12). The mission team then left Cyprus from the port of Paphos and sailed to the mainland of Pamphylia, arriving at Perga, a little inland from the coast near present-day Antalya. It was here, or quite possibly on the coast before the inland trek over the Taurus mountains to Pisidian Antioch, that John Mark left them to return to Jerusalem which was probably his home city. No reason is given for his "desertion" (15:38).

However, when it came to planning a further missionary journey, revisiting the cities they had been to on their first journey, and where churches had been founded, Barnabas proposed taking John Mark, but Paul refused. Luke tells us that Paul did not think it "wise" to take John Mark, because he had deserted them in Pamphylia and had not "continued with them in the work" (15:38). Paul did not want a repeat of that previous desertion, but Barnabas wanted to give John Mark a fresh chance. One had his eye mostly on the work, the other on the person. Paul wanted no impediment

---

[3] See Patrick Whitworth, *Gospel of the Kingdom* (Durham: Sacristy Press, 2021), pp. 2ff.

to the mission; Barnabas wanted to rehabilitate John Mark whom he valued. Both had valid reasons for their standpoint, but the disagreement in which neither side would back down became heated. Luke reports such a sharp contention that they parted company.

All three would prove invaluable in the spread of the gospel, none more so than Paul, as an apostle, church planter, and theologian of the early church. According to tradition, Barnabas returned to Cyprus where he became a bishop or church leader, and where, like Paul, he was martyred by the now hostile Roman provincial and imperial authorities. Mark became the author of the Gospel that bears his name and was written before the others: so compelling in its racy narrative about the Kingdom of God and in presenting a completely different type of king, the Lord Jesus Christ. John Mark's relationship with Paul was later restored, although Paul always seems to have treated him like a novice (see 2 Timothy 4:11). Perhaps it was Barnabas's special talent that he saw the gifting in others despite any failure of character and set them on a path to become all they could be. An invaluable gift in life generally, and also in the church.

CHAPTER 2

The first martyr: Stephen

Acts 6:5,8–15; Acts 7:1—8:1

After its exponential and explosive growth, the church ran into some problems of size. Indeed, the issue is introduced by Luke with the words, "the number of disciples was increasing" (Acts 6:1). One of the consequences was the increased need for care of Jewish widows from two separate language and cultural groups: some Hellenist and some Hebrew. Favouritism was being shown: the Greek-speaking Jewish widows were not receiving the same amount of food as the Hebrew-speaking Jewish widows. As so often, Greek and Hebrew formed a dividing line. The Hellenic, Greek-speaking Jewish widows were being overlooked in preference to the Hebrew-speaking Jewish widows. Since the church had set its face against favouritism from the very beginning, and caring for widows was very much part of the true faith (see James 1:27; 2:1–9), this was a problem in need of an urgent solution if harmony was to exist, and the church was seen to do what it said.

The solution to this issue, wisely suggested by the apostles, was that they should not give up their responsibility for preaching and teaching in order to attend to the matter, but should instead appoint seven reliable men to take care of it. The suggestion was warmly accepted and seven men, known to be "full of the Spirit and wisdom", were sought and then appointed. Among the seven were two whom we shall consider: two co-stars of the early church, Stephen and Philip, both of whom are given much space in the narrative of the early church in Acts.

Having settled this issue of the fair distribution of food, the growth of the church resumed. Right away Luke tells us "the word of God spread", numbers "increased rapidly", and "a large number of priests became obedient to the faith" (6:7). But not surprisingly, the growth of the church also attracted jealousy, envy, and persecution. When Stephen, as "a man full of grace and power did great wonders and miraculous signs (*sēmeîa megála*) among the people", opposition grew. It grew in particular from a distinct synagogue of Jews from Cyrene, Alexandria, Cilicia and Asia (6:9). This community was called the Synagogue of the Freedmen, who were presumably drawn from quite diverse parts of the Jewish *diaspora*, namely North Africa and Asia. What they may have had in common was that they were freed slaves from the Roman Empire. As James Dunn makes clear, these areas had the highest concentrations of Jews in the Eastern Empire.[4]

Among the many visitors assembled in Jerusalem at this time, it seems that Stephen especially mingled with these Jews from the *diaspora*. They were more conservatively inclined, by which we mean traditionalist, and the Temple to which they were especially committed appears to have been a point of debate with Stephen. At some stage this controversy reached boiling point.

Stephen's speech before the Sanhedrin

The Jews from the Synagogue of the Freedmen were determined to force the issue, and, incensed by Stephen's teaching, and perhaps intimidated by the great signs that God was doing through him, appealed for adjudication from the Sanhedrin. This was the same body that only some 18 months before had tried Jesus (Matthew 26:57–68).[5] There must have been some sense of *dêjá vu* among the assembled leaders. Here was a man who was a follower of Jesus performing many great signs and seemingly speaking a similar message. And, as at the trial of Jesus, the crowd was stirred up by false rumours (6:12). Once again false witnesses were produced to give evidence and to charge Stephen with the reported statement that the Temple would be destroyed and

---

[4]   Dunn, *Beginning from Jerusalem*, p. 258, footnote 72.

[5]   Dunn, *Beginning from Jerusalem*, p. 257.

the Law of Moses superseded (6:14, see also Matthew 26:59–63 and Mark 13:1,2). Hence the charge against Stephen was the same as they had been against Jesus: namely speaking about the destruction of the Temple. Members of the Synagogue of the Freedmen, being traditionalist at heart, violently objected to this. To cap it all, when the Sanhedrin looked over at the defendant in the dock, they saw that "his face was like the face of an angel" (6:15). Hence for some in the Sanhedrin there would have been a sense of foreboding. They might have had that same sinking feeling, and that same sense they were on the wrong side, as when they had confronted Jesus.

The High Priest asked whether the charges against Stephen were true, and it is at this point that Stephen began his lengthy speech. His retelling of the history of Israel is entirely orthodox until the very last few sentences (7:48–53). He relates the call of Abraham and the patriarchs, especially Joseph; the time of servitude in Egypt; the deliverance under Moses; the wanderings in the desert and the worship of Israel, first in a tabernacle (7:44,45) and then in the Temple built under Solomon. At this point, Stephen begins his argument that God is not restricted to a Temple. He quotes Isaiah: "'Heaven is my throne, and earth is my footstool. What kind of house will you build for me?' says the Lord. 'Or where will my resting place be? Has not my hand made all these things?'" (66:1,2).

There is now a change in the tone of Stephen's address (7:51ff.). He moves from a retelling of the story of Israel to an indictment of those conservative Jews who believe that the Temple and its worship were central to the future story of Israel, to the exclusion of the Messiah who had come in the person of Christ. Stephen puts his finger on an ancient division in Judaism between the prophetic stream and the liturgy of the Temple. Repeatedly, the prophets attack the vain repetition of Temple ceremonies and festivals which Israel uses as an insurance policy against true fulfilment of the Law and the requirement of obedience and compassion. Amos puts this contrast vividly when he says positively, on the one hand, "seek good, not evil, that you may live. Then the LORD God Almighty will be with you, just as you say he is. Hate evil, love good: maintain justice in the courts." And then negatively, on the other: "I hate, I despise your religious feasts; I cannot stand your assemblies. Even though you bring me burnt offerings and grain offerings, I will not accept them . . . Away with the noise of your songs! I will not listen to the music of your harps. But let justice roll on like a river, righteousness like a never-failing stream!" (Amos 5:14,15,21–23). Israel repeatedly paid more attention to the ceremonies, sacrifices and music performed in the Temple than to the radical fulfilment of the Law.

But as Jesus reiterates, God desires mercy and compassion (see Hosea 6:6 and Matthew 9:13) rather than the feasts and ceremonies of the Temple, insincerely fulfilled (see the Cleansing of the Temple in John 2:13ff.; Matthew 21:12ff.; Mark 11:12ff.).[6] Once again Stephen accuses the conservative Jews of the Synagogue of the Freedmen, and no doubt many in the Sanhedrin as well, of preferring to maintain the Temple tradition at all costs rather than obey the spirit of the Law. (The Temple had recently been extensively renovated and refurbished by Herod the Great over a period of 37 years.) Stephen concludes his speech by accusing his listeners thus: "You . . . have received the law that was put into effect through angels but have not obeyed it" (7:53). Worse, they have murdered the Righteous One predicted by the prophets (7:52). In these few sentences Stephen manages to provoke his audience and move them from listening attentively to an orthodox retelling of the story of Israel to fury at being identified as the ones who set in motion the judicial killing or murder of Jesus, and as those who preferred the ceremonies and religion of the Temple to keeping the Law and pursuing true justice. They are enraged, and they grind their teeth and resolve to stone him.

Even as their anger grows, Stephen, we are told, looks up and is granted a vision of heaven. He sees the glory of God and Jesus standing at the right hand of God (Acts 7:55, Revelation 1:12ff.). He cries out, "Look, I see heaven open and the Son of Man standing at the

---

[6]   Patrick Whitworth, *Gospel of Fulfilment: Exploring the Gospel of Matthew* (Durham: Sacristy Press, 2019), pp. 117ff.

right hand of God." It is the last thing the Sanhedrin want to hear: that the one whom they crucified for calling himself the Son of God is now standing at the right hand of God. For them it is blasphemy, but for Stephen it is the truth: the reality of how things are in the universe. The Sanhedrin cover their ears, yell at the tops of their voices and drag Stephen outside the city (Luke 23:32,33; Hebrews 13:12). They cannot bear to hear anything other than that Jesus was not the Messiah, but a blasphemer. They take Stephen outside and at a particular place they stone him. It is a brutal sentence which they are not too squeamish to enact. After all, the same Sanhedrin had wanted the Roman Governor Pilate to pronounce judgement on Jesus so that he would be crucified, but in this case, they take the administration of the law and the death penalty into their own hands and perform the stoning themselves.

Stephen dies like Jesus: praying that God will not let this sin stand against his persecutors (7:60; Luke 23:34), committing his spirit into the hands of Jesus (Luke 23:46), and in his case, falling asleep. Perhaps as the stones hit his body and his head, he is enveloped in unconsciousness, which shields him from further pain and draws him fully into the Father's presence.

So, Stephen dies as the first martyr of the Christian era. Stephen's feast day is celebrated by the Church the day after Christmas on December 26 and as Augustine said "Just as Christ by being born was joined to Stephen, so Stephen by dying was joined to Christ." (Sermon

330). There will be a multitude of martyrs to come through the next three centuries of the Roman period, through the treatment of one part of the church by the other, during the missionary movements of the eighteenth and nineteenth centuries; through the persecution by communism in Russia, Eastern Europe, China, and North Korea; and by Islam, especially in Iran, Pakistan, and Egypt. Tertullian famously said that the "blood of the martyrs is the seed of the church", and in the book of Revelation martyrs are identified as a noble cohort in heaven (7:9–17; 12:11). Stephen's understanding that the role of the Temple has been superseded by Jesus and his single eternal sacrifice (Hebrews 10:11–14), thereby making the whole priestly and sacrificial system redundant, is something the Sanhedrin cannot countenance. They block their ears and close their minds, but it cannot change the reality of things. One bystander, looking after the coats as others get down to the terrible business of hurling stones at their defenceless victim, may himself have been struck by Stephen's demeanour. In just a few weeks he too will have a vision of Christ and hear Christ's voice, and his life will be transformed for ever (8:1). His name is Saul.

CHAPTER 3

The evangelist: Philip

Acts 6:1–7; 8:1–40; 21:1–9

Philip is the second of the magnificent seven (Acts 6:5,6) to be given full credit for his extraordinary ministry in the narrative of the Acts of the Apostles. Stephen and Philip are clearly the principal ministers of this illustrious group. After the death of Stephen, a general persecution appears to have broken out in Jerusalem with the effect of scattering the church far outside the city, and into surrounding regions (8:1). At the forefront of this persecution is Saul (Paul) who now goes from house to house dragging both men and women off to prison (8:3; Galatians 1:13). Despite the persecution, the apostles stay in Jerusalem, perhaps not yet fully understanding the imperative to take the gospel to "Samaria and to the ends of the earth" (1:8). It may have been that the persecution was primarily directed against the Hellenist Jews, which may account for the dispersal of the Seven and for the apostles (who were

Hebrew Jews) being left unmolested for the moment in Jerusalem.[7]

What follows in the account of Philip's ministry is a remarkable fulfilment of Jesus's words that the church will take the gospel to Samaria and then to the ends of the earth (1:8). Indeed, the persecution that follows the martyrdom of Stephen spreads the seed of the church like spores shaken from a sunflower in the wind. Soon we see that those spores of the word travel to Samaria, Ethiopia, Phoenicia, Cyprus and Antioch (see 8:1–40; 11:19–21). Along with the preaching of Peter to the Jews of the *diaspora* on the Day of Pentecost (2:7–12), this persecution creates a new dynamic and energy for evangelism not previously seen. Philip's role in this is to take the gospel to Samaria and, through a high official of Queen Candace of Ethiopia, to Ethiopia as well.

The healing of the breach with Samaria

To understand the importance of this movement of the gospel, we must fully grasp the great gulf that existed between Judah (or the Southern Kingdom) and Samaria.

This split between Samaria and the Southern Kingdom occurred after the death of Solomon and the accession of his headstrong son Rehoboam (*c.*931–913 BC), and his harsh policies towards his subjects, especially the northern tribes (see 1 Kings 12, especially v. 14). This led

---

[7]   Dunn, *Beginning from Jerusalem*, p. 277, 278.

to their secession from Judah or the Southern Kingdom. Led by Jeroboam, an important official of Solomon, a new government was set up in Samaria to lead the ten tribes of Northern Israel; all the tribes of Israel, that is, except Judah and Benjamin in the south.

A new idolatrous cult was set up by Jeroboam at Bethel and Dan (1 Kings 12:25–33). This cult revolved around the worship of golden calves and mimicked the timing of festivals in Jerusalem. In this way, Jeroboam hoped to consolidate his hold over the ten tribes. Instead, he led them into an idolatry from which they did not depart and for which they would pay a heavy price. A succession of evil, or just plain bad kings followed, despite the interventions of numerous prophets, such as Elijah, Elisha, Amos, and Hosea, until, in *c.*724 BC, the Assyrians invaded and took over the country (see 2 Kings 17). Many of the northern tribes were then taken into exile, scattered permanently in present-day northern Iraq, while other peoples from the Assyrian Empire were settled among a remnant in Samaria where they worshipped their own gods in different towns (see 2 Kings 17:29ff.). Israel thus became a deeply hybrid nation. And, as renewal followed in the Southern Kingdom after the return from Exile in Babylon in *c.*445 BC, the gulf between north and south only widened.

During Jesus's ministry, the separation between Samaria (as it was now called) and Judah was deep, seemingly beyond repair. But Jesus did not ignore the Samaritans. Both Luke and John tell us about Jesus's attitude towards them. Luke tells us that Jesus makes a Samaritan the hero of his story about the man who fell among thieves on the road from Jerusalem to Jericho (Luke 10:25–37). Indeed, Luke places this parable directly after his teaching about mission, making, therefore, the Good Samaritan an exemplary missionary. Likewise, John tells us in his introduction to Jesus's conversation with the Samaritan woman at the well that "Jews do not associate with Samaritans" (John 4:9). Jesus, however, is not prepared to turn his back on the people living in Samaria but brings them salvation (John 4:10–15) and indeed many drank from "the well of salvation" having heard the woman's testimony (John 4:39–42). It is not surprising, therefore, that Jesus's plan for the evangelization of the world should specifically include Samaria (see Acts 1:8). With the persecution of the church in Jerusalem, the moment had come for the fulfilment of this plan.

Luke's account in Acts begins plainly enough, "Philip went down to a city in Samaria and proclaimed the Christ [or Messiah] there." Perhaps the area was close to Sychar where the woman at the well had met Jesus and where many believed (John 4:5,39). Certainly, if the woman was still alive, and most likely she was, the news of Philip's coming would have struck a chord. His preaching of Jesus being the Christ would have chimed with what she herself believed and knew, and what many others from her community had found (4:25,26). A combination of Philip's persuasive speaking and the miraculous signs performed through him had a powerful effect on the community. Many evil spirits were driven out, many paralytics and cripples were healed, and we are told, "there was great joy in that city" (Acts 8:8). But the evidence of this power attracted not only the curious but also the manipulative, and one such person was Simon Magus.

Simon Magus

Simon Magus, or Simon the Magician, was already well known in Samaria where people were impressed by his feats of magic (8:9). This power had given him popularity and acclaim. In fact, the people went so far as to say, "This man is the divine power known as the Great Power" (8:10). When Philip came to the region Simon also believed, although given what followed later, one has to question his sincerity. Rather like Elymas in Cyprus (13:8) and the fortune-telling girl in Philippi (16:17), people already used to occult power were fascinated by the power of God. In each case they followed either Philip or Paul around, perhaps seeking a slice of this novel supernatural action. But it seems they were more interested in finding power than in submitting themselves to Christ.

The mission to Samaria marked a significant advance of the gospel into greater Israel (before moving further afield into the Gentile world). It was deemed important enough for the apostles in Jerusalem to come and pray for the new Samaritan converts, and especially that they might receive the Holy Spirit who had not yet been given to them. So, Peter and John went down to Samaria to pray in this way and these converts received the Spirit and quite probably demonstrated this by using spiritual gifts of either tongues or prophecy. When Simon saw that the Spirit was given through the laying on of hands, he made the mistake of asking Peter whether he could acquire this gift or power with money. This was the second incident where money had affected spiritual vision in the Acts. (Earlier Ananias and Sapphira had pretended to give all the money acquired from the sale of property to the apostles, yet had retained some secretly for themselves. There had been no compulsion for them to give all their money, but they pretended to do so while keeping some for themselves. For such hypocrisy there was harsh judgement.)

Now, when he saw the power of God given freely to the Samaritans, Simon sought to use money to buy that power for himself. He was severely rebuked by the Apostle Peter, using the authority given to him (see Matthew 16:17–20) by Jesus, and told to repent, in the hope that he might find forgiveness and that nothing worse should befall him. We are not told whether Simon did so, but according to church tradition and the writings of Irenaeus, Hippolytus and the heresy-hunter Epiphanius, Bishop of Salamis in Cyprus, Simon, far from turning back into the way of salvation as described by the apostles, became the father of Gnosticism, a heresy that became one of the biggest challenges for the early Christian churches. As far as the narrative of Acts is concerned, the story reverts to Philip and his call to share the gospel with the first Gentile in the account.

The Ethiopian eunuch

There could not have been a better prepared moment of personal evangelism. Philip, although a gifted evangelist, is given every assistance in the conversion of this first-named Gentile in the Acts of the Apostles.

Firstly, an angel directs Philip, telling him to go down to the desert road from Jerusalem to Gaza. This would have been the road from Jerusalem to the coast that joined up with the Via Maris, which was the main trade route from Egypt to Syria and Anatolia. It may be that Philip found the chariot of the Ethiopian on the stretch of road between Jerusalem and Via Maris. The Ethiopian was the treasurer of the Queen of Ethiopia, whose title was Candace. Her surname may have been Amantitere (*c.*AD 25–41), and she ruled over Nubia, a land stretching from Southern Egypt and Sudan to Ethiopia and comprising Nilo-Saharan ethnic peoples. The Ethiopian eunuch was returning from Jerusalem, having gone there for a festival as a Gentile worshipper. As a Gentile, he would have been restricted to the Court of the Gentiles at the Temple, and as a eunuch he would have been unable to enter the assembly of the Lord (Deuteronomy 23:1). Thus, he was seeking the Lord but under those current Jewish arrangements was prevented from full inclusion into the people of God. All that was about to change.

The Ethiopian had bought a precious and expensive hand-copied manuscript or scroll of the prophet Isaiah. Given that the first editions of the Gospels would not even be in circulation before AD 65 at the earliest, some 30 years thereafter, the Ethiopian could not have chosen a better book in the Old Testament. Isaiah speaks mostly about the work of the Messiah in terms of the Servant Songs (Isaiah 42:1–9; 49:1–13; 50:4–11; 52:13—53:12; 61:1–4), the Suffering Servant (Isaiah 52:1—53:12), and the coming of Immanuel (Isaiah 9:1–7; 11).

So, when Philip draws alongside the chariot, he hears the Ethiopian reading aloud what is probably one of the most important passages in the Old Testament, the passage about the redemptive sufferings of the Messiah, also called the Suffering Servant. But what the Ethiopian needs is someone to explain the significance of these sufferings: who it is that is suffering, and for what purpose, and how these sufferings can be connected to his own life. Philip can do all these things. He joins the Ethiopian in his chariot and sitting beside him explains what his companion needs to know. Philip tells him "the good news about Jesus" (8:35), using the very passage that the Ethiopian has just read. The Ethiopian, like others in Acts (e.g. Lydia), believes. His heart is opened, his mind grasps the significance of what he is being told, and seeing some water he asks if he might be baptized. Clearly, he is a decisive man, who accepts the truth and immediately acts upon it, and it is this quality presumably, among others, that has enabled him to reach such a high position. Almost certainly he would have started a church in Nubia, thus making the region one of the first to accept Christianity outside Israel.

Meanwhile, the supernatural direction of Philip continues. He suddenly finds himself caught up by the Spirit and conveyed north to Azotus (8:39). We then see Philip conducting missions in all the communities between Azotus (Ashdod) and Caesarea in the north of the country, where he eventually settles. Later in Acts, we find Philip still there: married and with four unmarried daughters who prophesy when Paul arrives on his final journey to Jerusalem (21:8,9).

Philip, as one of the Seven, proved a remarkable evangelist, but nevertheless his ministry to the Samaritans required the imprimatur of the apostles to mark each new stage of the outreach from Jerusalem to the ends of the earth (1:8). Through the laying on of hands by Peter and John, the Spirit was given (8:17; 10:44). The more formal entry of the Gentiles into the church would, however, be marked not by Philip speaking to the Ethiopian and seeing his conversion (and presumably the receipt of the Spirit), but by Peter's visit to Cornelius to which we will come. But before we do so, Acts records the remarkable conversion of Saul (Paul) and the vital role of Ananias in that event.

CHAPTER 4

The go-between: Ananias

Acts 9:10–19

We would never have heard of Ananias had it not been for his role in welcoming and including Saul (Paul) into the church at Damascus. He was the vital link in the chain of events that followed Saul's conversion (a better word might be *fulfilment* rather than conversion), which took place on the road to Damascus where Saul had gone to arrest and detain Christian Jews. The High Priest had given Saul authority to do this and men to help him detain what may well have been a large number of Christians, for there was a large Jewish community in Damascus (Acts 9:1,2).

En route to Damascus Saul had an incontrovertible vision of Christ and heard his voice. Through this demonstration of divine power Saul was left lying on the ground, temporarily blinded, thrown from his horse or mule, trying to take in the significance of the heavenly voice that accused him of persecuting Jesus (9:3–8). He was aware that he was being directly addressed by Jesus, the one he was attacking in the lives of his followers. For three days Saul remained blind, not eating any food, fasting, and thinking through the revolutionary implications of what had happened.

All Saul's previous assumptions have now been overturned. He can no longer consider Jesus a blaspheming Rabbi who despised the Law and the Prophets. In light of this vision, Saul has to change completely his estimation of Jesus and to start to believe that he is the Messiah, crucified and now risen.

Nevertheless, Saul is blind, surrounded by men who do not understand what has happened, who have heard a voice but have seen no light or vision. They are speechless and probably helpless. And the Christian community is in fear of Saul whom they rightly believe had only come to arrest them (see 9:1,2). How is Saul to be included in the Christian community in Damascus and further afield? Who will welcome him into the Christian family? Who will pray for him to receive his sight back and be filled with the Spirit? Who will baptize him into the Christian faith, that he might become a follower of the Way which only days before he had been violently attacking? There must be someone to act as a link in the chain, a go-between, and a bridge to a new life and destiny. That person is Ananias, who will be written into the Christian story as one of its humble, exemplary heroes.

The reluctant missionary

The theatre group "Riding Lights" have a marvellously vivid sketch, typical of their work, of Ananias and his wife in bed, wearing tasselled night-caps, and being woken by this vision and commission, and hoping it is a terrible mistake. To be suddenly addressed by the Lord is fearful enough, but here this is compounded by an instruction that goes beyond belief. Ananias is to go to the house of Judas in Straight Street; there he will find Saul, a man from Tarsus, who is praying and who has himself received a vision in which he sees a man called Ananias come and pray for him that his sight might be restored. It all seems so far-fetched. Ananias might already have been warned to be careful and that Christians were in danger of their lives because Saul was coming to Damascus. But now God is sending him to the self-same Saul to restore his sight: surely the better to see who to arrest!

Ananias is deferential but hesitant. He is an understandably reluctant missionary as far as this task was concerned. Could there be a crossed wire? Is the Lord properly informed about Saul? Does he really know the gravity of the situation? In case God has forgotten, Ananias briefs him thus: "I have heard many reports about this man and all the harm he has done to your saints in Jerusalem. And he has come here with authority from the chief priests to arrest all who call upon your name" (9:13,14). But God's reply is unambiguous and reveals more of his plan.

God's plan revealed

The Lord's response is unequivocal, as it so often is, for he knows the end from the beginning. "Go!" he says to Ananias. It is a direct command. God then gives Ananias additional insight to spur him on. He shares his plan for Saul (see John 15:15). As amazing and surprising as it must have sounded, Ananias is told, "This man is my chosen instrument to carry my name before the Gentiles and their kings and before the people of Israel. I will show him how much he must suffer for my name" (9:15,16).

Choosing the chief persecutor of the church as the primary advocate of the gospel to the powerbrokers of his generation was both a masterstroke and an extraordinary change of affairs. Saul was to be God's chosen instrument. It must have been hard for Ananias to grasp the significance of this in just a few moments, or for him to understand the change that had come over Saul and what this meant for the Christians in Damascus. But for this plan to work out, Ananias now has to go to Straight Street and welcome and pray for Saul. (Straight Street is still to be found in Damascus—I went there in 2002 before the outbreak of the catastrophic Syrian civil war.) So, after his initial misgivings, Ananias obediently leaves his house and makes his way to Straight Street where Saul is praying. When he enters the house of Judas, Ananias finds a blind, fasting and praying Saul, which must have reassured him that he had heard God rightly and that what he was about to do was not folly or madness, but simply the completion of what God himself had begun on the Damascus Road.

Brother Saul

What is so striking about this meeting is the opening address of Ananias to Saul. Ananias begins with, "Brother Saul" (9:17). This is the man who just days before had been commissioned to imprison Christians, and worse, who is now blind, praying, and waiting meekly to discover the next steps in his spiritual journey. But more than that, Ananias recognizes that Saul is now his brother through the grace of God. They are in an entirely new relationship which transcends everything that has gone before. For now, and for ever, Jew and Gentile, slave and free, male and female are one in Christ (Galatians 3:28). Saul has become part of the family of God. He has also been shown in a vision that Ananias will come and place his hands on him and pray for the restoration of his sight (Acts 9:12). That moment has now come. Ananias lays his hands on Saul, tells him that he is doing what Jesus has instructed him to do, and prays for both the restoration of Saul's sight and the filling of the Spirit. Saul's sight is restored. He is filled with God's Spirit and straightway is baptized. In just a few eventful moments, Saul has completed his transfer into the Christian community. He truly belongs in this community and is qualified by Jesus.

Just sometimes we are called to change our minds about something or someone: a person in the church, someone in our family, a situation which confronts us, and to do so in a radical way. This is what Ananias had to do upon hearing the voice of God: he must have the grace to obey, and the courage to put God's command into action. He is the link in the chain between God's address to Saul on the Damascus Road and the fulfilment of his calling as Apostle to the Gentiles and the teacher of the church. Ananias is a small but vital link in the story of salvation that is coming to the world.

CHAPTER 5

The God-fearing centurion: Cornelius

Acts 10:1–48

Centurions have a universally good press in the Gospels and the Acts of the Apostles. Indeed, no professional group is praised more in the New Testament. Jesus says of the centurion in Luke's Gospel that he has "not found such great faith even in Israel" (Luke 7:9). Later in Luke's Gospel, as in the other synoptic Gospels, the centurion overseeing the crucifixion of Jesus says, "Surely this was a righteous man" (Luke 23:47). In Mark, the Greek is stronger and the centurion says: "Surely this man was the Son of God (*uios theoū*)" (Mark 15:39), thus making a Christian profession.

Furthermore, centurions appear to be on the side of the angels. Cornelius is devout and God-fearing, as we shall see (Acts 10:2). Another Roman officer called a *chiliarch*—a commander of thousands—saves Paul from mob attack when he is addressing the crowd outside the Temple in Jerusalem (Acts 21:27ff.). The mob is already suspicious of Paul for not teaching full compliance with the Jewish Law and is also suspicious that he has brought Greeks into the Temple area (Acts 21:28). They want to attack him. But the commander permits Paul to speak to the crowd, which he does. However, when Paul comes to the part of his address where he describes being sent to the Gentiles by God himself, the crowd once more becomes enraged and threatens to stone him. The chiliarch snatches him from the jaws of this fate, but then threatens him with flogging and interrogation. So, Paul pleads his Roman citizenship and at this the centurion in charge of the flogging party stands his soldiers down (Acts 22:25–29).

Other centurions will effectively guard Paul, thus ensuring his transfer to Rome where he will be tried and bear witness (Acts 23:11). Centurions will escort him from Jerusalem to Caesarea and frustrate an ambush to kill him (Acts 23:12–35). And when Paul's ship capsizes and runs aground off Malta, the centurion heeds Paul's warning and prevents the soldiers killing the prisoners, and instead encourages them all to swim for shore (Acts 27:43).

Of all the centurions, however, the one who has the most significant role in the spreading out of the gospel is Cornelius. He is the main representative of the Gentile world in the movement of the gospel from Jerusalem, Judea and Samaria into the Gentile parts of the Roman Empire. Although the conversion of the Ethiopian eunuch seems to have been the first conversion of a

Gentile in the Acts, we can't be sure of the chronology. It is the preaching of the gospel by the leading apostle, Peter, to a gathered Gentile audience, and the consequent gift of the Spirit that seems to be the main step-change in the mission of the church outside its original Jewish and Semitic cradle (Acts 2:1–41).

Cornelius was a centurion based in Caesarea. Like Jerusalem, the city had undergone an extensive refit by Herod the Great (72–4 BC) who was the sole ruler of Judea from 37 BC.

This refit of the city included a new harbour, renamed after Caesar Augustus. Caesarea became one of the most important cities in Palestine. The Roman Prefect resided there, as did the main garrison in Judea, of which Cornelius's centurion was a part. Legions in this period comprised 4,800 legionnaires made up of ten cohorts of six centuries each (a century being 80 soldiers and a cohort being 480). Cornelius's centurion was known as the Italian Regiment. It is possible that part of the legion was based in Caesarea, with other parts, when not on campaign, garrisoned in Antioch and Jerusalem. Or it could be that Cornelius had by now retired and was living in Caesarea with his family and friends.[8] Cornelius was a man of real piety and known as a God-fearer (see Psalm 111:10; Proverbs 1:7). He feared God, was drawn to Judaism, prayed constantly, and gave money to the poor regularly (Acts 10:1–3).

---

[8]   Dunn, *Beginning from Jerusalem*, p. 390.

Not only this, but his own piety and faith influenced his whole household.

One day when Cornelius is praying an angel appears to him. Angels were the regular heralds of a new era of God's work. They were there at the Exodus; they were there at the giving of the Law (Acts 7:53; Galatians 3:19). They galvanized prophetic witness (Isaiah 6:2); they announced the coming of the Messiah (Luke 1:26; 2:9–15); they were there at the resurrection (Matthew 28:2–7; John 20:12,13); and they were there at the ascension (Acts 1:10).

An angel now appears to Cornelius as the herald of an impending new age for the gospel. The angel gives him specific encouragement and instructions. Cornelius's prayers and giving have been noted by God, his gifts are like a sweet memorial. After this angelic message, Cornelius sends men to Joppa to fetch Simon, known as Peter, who is staying in a house by the sea with another Simon, a tanner (Acts 10:4–6). Despite the sudden surprise of being addressed by an angel, Cornelius has a clear enough head to remember the instruction and tells two of his servants, together with "a devout soldier", to go to Joppa and fetch Peter and bring him back.

Meanwhile Peter was on a mission to the coastal plain of Israel. Amongst other places, Peter ministered particularly in Lydda and Joppa. Lydda was on the road from Jerusalem to Joppa which is on the coast. In Lydda, God healed Aeneas, who had been paralysed for eight years (Acts 9:33). As a result, many turned to the Lord.

When a much-loved Christian called Tabitha died in Joppa, the Christians there, hearing that Peter was nearby in Lydda, sent for him. In a miracle reminiscent of Jesus's healing of Jairus's daughter (Mark 5:37–43), which Peter himself had witnessed, Peter prayed for Tabitha who came back to life.

And now, while Peter is resting at the house of Simon the Tanner, two simultaneous events occur. First, while he is waiting for lunch, he has a vision of a sheet being let down from heaven in which are all kinds of animals, both clean and unclean, and a command from God to eat (10:10–16). And secondly, while Peter is objecting in his vision that some of the meat is unclean, there is another synchronized event. With impeccable, indeed supernatural, timing there is a knock at the door and Cornelius's servants tell of their master's encounter with an angel and ask Peter to go back with them to Cornelius's house in Caesarea. It is belt-and-braces revelation: unmistakeable however, revolutionary. With such prompts Peter can hardly refuse! Having heard the voice of the Spirit to go with these men, Peter makes preparations to accompany them the next day (10:19–23).

By the time Peter arrives, Cornelius has gathered his relatives and close friends at his house, and they are expectantly waiting to hear Peter's message. On his arrival, Cornelius pays Peter undue deference, bordering on obeisance, and falls at his feet. But Peter is quick to remind him that he is only mortal (10:26). Peter goes into the house and addresses the company, first sharing, somewhat negatively, how his faith usually forbids from sharing fellowship with Gentiles. Peter then explains that God has intervened through a vision to show him that there must now be no discrimination between Jew and Gentile (10:28). Cornelius then repeats his own encounter with an angel and how he was told to send to Joppa for Peter (10:30–33). In response, Peter reiterates that God does not show favouritism, "but accepts men from every nation". He begins a discursive narrative about the ministry of Jesus, who "God anointed . . . with the Holy Spirit and power, and how he went around doing good and healing all who were under the power of the devil", men, women and children (10:38). Peter then recalls the crucifixion and resurrection of Jesus and the message that he commanded the apostles to preach. It is a message that God has made Jesus judge of the living and the dead and "that everyone who believes in him receives forgiveness of sins through his name" (10:43).

At this point, God breaks in and the Holy Spirit is given to the Gentiles just as the Spirit was poured out (2:17,33) on the people in Jerusalem on the Day of Pentecost. This is an undeniable, perceptible, observable, irreversible event. Peter's audience is sovereignly blessed by the Spirit and given gifts of tongues and praise. Those with Peter who are witnesses of the event and are themselves faithful circumcised members of Israel see that those without the Law or circumcision are now included directly by God in the New Covenant and the community of the church, and they are amazed (10:45)! Seeing this turn of events and all that has preceded it by way of preparation, Peter reaches the right conclusion that no-one can "keep these people from being baptized with water" as they have already received the Holy Spirit. The people are baptized in the name of Jesus Christ and received into the church. This is a major staging post in the mission of the church and the fulfilment of God's eternal plan, as Paul himself reflects on in Ephesians 2:11–13. Cornelius, the God-fearing, humble, generous, open-hearted centurion has seen and experienced a greater advance of the gospel than he ever did of Roman arms. There is to be no partiality in the church of the New Covenant, with Gentile and Jew now members of the body of Christ *together*.

CHAPTER 6

The prophet: Agabus

Acts 11:19–30; 21:1–16

Prophecy was part of the life of the early church, just as it was part of the life of Israel. In the Old Testament, several prophets bestride the narrative of Israel like colossi, and in particular Isaiah, Jeremiah and Ezekiel, who shaped the consciousness of Israel and Judah around the time of the Exile: foretelling the events of Judah's fall and captivity, shaping their response to these events as well as upbraiding their failures or giving a far-off glimpse of the future and the coming of the Messiah (see Isaiah 9:1–7; 52:13—53:12). Other prophets, like Elijah and Elisha, were godly signposts in days of idolatry and backsliding from Israel's vocation. Yet more prophets brought similar short and vivid messages to an erring kingdom (Jonah, Habakkuk and Haggai) and also to nearby nations: Tyre, Egypt and Lebanon, Moab and Edom (see Ezekiel 26 ff.). Daniel in particular not only recalls the great life of a righteous man in exile in Babylon but receives a unique vision of the all-important Son-of-Man figure, which, alongside the Suffering Servant of Isaiah, Jesus would in time apply to himself.

With the coming of the Spirit prophecy did not cease. John the Baptist was in one sense the last of the Old Testament prophets. On the Day of Pentecost, and quoting Joel 2:28–32, Peter said, "In the last days, God says, I will pour out my Spirit on all people. Your sons and your daughters will prophesy, your young men will see visions, your old men will dream dreams" (Acts 2:17). And this is what happened. The Spirit was given to all who believed in Christ and they all called upon the name of the Lord (Acts 2:38). So, prophets were to be found in the early church. There were prophets and teachers in the church at Antioch (13:1). Philip the evangelist had four unmarried daughters who prophesied (21:9), and there was Agabus who appears on two important occasions in the book of Acts (11:28; 21:11).

Later in the New Testament, Paul explains the significance of prophecy. It is given by the Holy Spirit to the body of Christ for direction and upbuilding and is received individually. It is a highly desirable gift (1 Corinthians 14:1) and, properly used, can "strengthen, encourage and comfort" (1 Corinthians 14:3–5). A message of prophecy should be carefully evaluated or "weighed" by the body of Christ to assess its validity, and its message heeded (1 Corinthians 14:29). Prophecy can also have an evangelistic effect: laying bare the secrets of people's hearts (1 Corinthians 14:24,25). The value of prophecy lies especially in its specific application to an individual, church or community. Agabus is a good example of this the two times he appears in the Acts of the Apostles.

The first mention of Agabus is in the church at Antioch. This mega church, which emerged rapidly because of the scattering of persecuted Christians to Antioch and elsewhere, became a strong missionary church with a large Hellenist contingent. Saul was taken by Barnabas from Tarsus to Antioch (11:25,26) and together they taught the church there. During this time a group of prophets came down from Jerusalem, and one of them, Agabus, stood up and gave an important prophecy.

Agabus predicts a "severe famine would spread over the entire Roman world" (11:28) and that this will happen in the reign of Claudius. This prophecy, and the consequent gift of money to the church in Judea, is thought to have happened in AD 46/47.[9] This would have fallen squarely in the reign of Claudius (AD 41–54), who became emperor after the assassination of Caligula. A famine is indeed known to have occurred at this time in Judea in AD 45/46 and Agabus is referring to its ongoing consequences. Although at this distance it is difficult to be precise about timing and dates, it seems that Agabus's prophecy was made before the worst of the famine,

---

[9] Wright, *Paul: A Biography*, p. 433, Timeline/Chronology.

and that the church in Antioch took action. They sent their gifts to Jerusalem with Saul and Barnabas, thereby strengthening the fellowship between these two principal churches of the region, and indeed of the early Christian movement. In fact, the sending of money in time of need, from the richer to poorer churches, may well have started as a result of this particular prophecy. Later Paul would make the distribution of money to poorer churches from the richer Hellenic ones central to his ministry. Money was taken to the struggling communities of Judea (see Romans 15:23ff.; 2 Corinthians 8:1–7; 8:16ff.). Paul would expend much energy, struggle and ink upon this task.

What is clear from these accounts in Acts is the importance accorded prophecy in the early church in terms of forming strategy and directing resources. When Paul said that the church was built upon the five-fold ministry of the Spirit, which included apostles, prophets, evangelists, pastors and teachers, this was a type of prophecy in itself (Ephesians 4:11). It was a prophecy of which he had first-hand experience. It directed his own steps and would become an enduring part of a Spirit-led church.

The second occasion Luke records Agabus prophesying comes in Acts 21 and once again concerns Paul, only even more personally and towards the end of his ministry. In c.AD 59, Paul travels back from Corinth to Jerusalem at the end of his third missionary journey. He revisits Philippi before sailing to Troas, Assos,

Miletus, Rhodes, Tyre, Ptolemais, and then Caesarea (Acts 21:1–9). In Caesarea, he stays with Philip and his four prophesying daughters. While he is there Agabus visits, and in a dramatic act takes Paul's belt from him and ties his own hands and feet, saying: "The Holy Spirit says, 'In this way the Jews of Jerusalem will bind the owner of this belt and will hand him over to the Gentiles'" (21:11). It must have been a dramatic moment and although the Spirit had been witnessing to Paul all along the route that he would face opposition in Jerusalem, this represented a further heightening of tension. Indeed, the style of this prophecy from Agabus is reminiscent of something from the Old Testament, where often a visual sign is given or enacted by the prophet, as in Jeremiah buying a field, for example, or Jeremiah wearing a linen belt (Jeremiah 32 and 13:1ff.). In this instance, Agabus is simply enacting what will happen to Paul when he arrives in Jerusalem: he will be bound and handed over to the Gentiles. It is an accurate prediction, not a direction to Paul to avoid this outcome. It is a forewarning, not a forbidding. In this way, the church will know that his arrest and trial are all part of God's plan and should not be alarmed (see Acts 9:15,16 and Philippians 1:12–14).

In these two ways, no doubt among many other prophecies, Agabus informs the church so that appropriate action can be taken or preparation made. These are both predictive types of prophecy that prove true. The ministry of Agabus and his prophetic gift are an integral part of the equipping of the church by the Spirit. Perhaps more often prophecy is simply a specific word of encouragement to the church to remain true to its calling in testing circumstances. Years later, in AD 374, in the first full-length book written about the Spirit, Basil of Caesarea writes, "The spirit bearing souls that are illuminated by the Spirit are themselves made spiritual, and they send forth grace to others. Thence comes foreknowledge of the future, understanding of mysteries, apprehension of secrets, distributions of graces, heavenly citizenship, the chorus with angels, unending joy, remaining in God, and the highest object of desire, becoming God."[10]

Surely Agabus would have agreed.

---

[10] Basil of Caesarea, *On the Holy Spirit* (Crestwood, NY: St Vladimir's Press, 2011), ch. 9, §9,23.

The chairman: James

*Acts 15:1–35; 21:17–26; Galatians
1:18– 24; The Epistle of James*

By now we are getting a feel for the wide variety of people who enabled the mission of God in the early church. They were to become more varied. Not only did these people have varied backgrounds, they also had different giftings that marked them out in the church and made for the variegated (*polupoíkilos*) grace of God (Ephesians 3:10). Soon we will include in our list an able, entrepreneurial businesswoman and a gifted married couple. But first we come to a man gifted to be the chairman of the first church council, the first of many councils stretching from Nicaea to Vatican II and beyond.

James is normally called "James, the Lord's brother" (see Galatians 1:19). However, it became common among writers like Jerome, Ambrose and Epiphanius of Salamis, among others, to maintain that Joseph had had a previous marriage from which Jesus's stepbrothers and -sisters came (they were not considered half-brothers, because of the virginal conception of Mary and her perpetual virginity). However, there is no obvious biblical evidence to support this. Jesus's family is quite often mentioned in the Gospels and his siblings are simply referred to as his brothers and sisters (Matthew 13:55,56; Mark 6:3; Luke 8:19–21; John 2:12; 7:2–5). The most natural explanation is that they were from the same family, although Jesus had a different conception and biological father (see Luke 1:34,35; Matthew 1:20). If James was the natural brother of Jesus, he was also called "James the Less" by the early church, distinguishing him from the Apostle James, the brother of John. James is also sometimes called "James the Great" or sometimes "James the Just" because of his writing (The Epistle of James) and his ascetic lifestyle. In the Greek-speaking church, he was called *adelphotheos*—brother of the Lord.

It appears that by virtue of his faith and gifting, James rose to occupy an important role in the Jerusalem church. Although he was not an apostle, his closeness to Jesus and his faith in him as the Son of God and Messiah meant that he was second only to Peter in the Jerusalem church. By the time of Saul's conversion in *c.*AD 33, it appears that James, along with Peter and John, were leaders there. Indeed, in Galatians 2:9, James (most probably *not* the brother of John) is mentioned first. Although not an apostle, it seems that he had acquired seniority through his gifts, wisdom and spiritual stature. And James would remain leader of the church in Jerusalem at least up to *c*.AD 58 when Paul was arrested in Jerusalem before his extensive trials (Acts 21:17ff.). These were all good characteristics in a chairman. And it became clear from the outset that the church not only needed occasions of worship and teaching, but also periods of collective administration led by a chairman. This was clearly James's gifting. And the most important occasion for his chairmanship was the Council of Jerusalem.

The Council of Jerusalem *c*.AD 48/49

The meeting for which James's chairmanship is well known is the Council of Jerusalem, which is described in Acts 15. The context was a sharp division in the church at Antioch, where there were many Gentile believers, over the need to observe the Jewish Law. Some men who came down to Antioch from Judea, and probably from Jerusalem, were insisting that unless people were circumcised "according to the custom taught by Moses" they could not be saved (15:1–2). This was a clear threat to the essence of the gospel, which is based on grace, and it led to a sharp dispute between these so called Judaizers and Paul and Barnabas. As it was not possible to settle the matter authoritatively in Antioch, the church sent Paul and Barnabas to seek a ruling on the matter from the apostles and elders in Jerusalem (15:2b). They travelled up to Jerusalem and told several Christian communities on the way about the fruitful mission they had just concluded among the Gentiles (15:2,3), news that made those communities very happy.

On arrival in Jerusalem, Paul and Barnabas were welcomed by the church, the apostles and the elders, and they told them of their fruitful mission. The apostles at Jerusalem had already heard from Simon Peter how the Gentiles were included in the New Covenant when the Spirit was given to them in the house of Cornelius. Indeed, Peter had already had to explain to the Jewish Christian party in Jerusalem why he had gone to the house of an uncircumcised Gentile (see Acts 11:1–18). But when he had told them "precisely" how it had all happened, and how God had included the Gentiles by his own sovereign act of giving them the Spirit, we are told that "the circumcised believers" rejoiced and praised God saying, "So then, God has granted even the Gentiles repentance unto life" (11:2,18).

Nevertheless, there were some of the "circumcised party", and in particular some who were now Christians but had formerly been Pharisees (15:5) and who came to be called Judaizers, who insisted that although Gentiles could be included in the community of the church they should *still observe* much, if not all, of the Mosaic Law with regard to the sabbath, circumcision and food laws. They baldly stated, "The Gentiles must be circumcised and required to obey the Law of Moses"

(15:5). The Council, it seems, heard the arguments of these Judaizers before they met together to consider the issues.

When the Council subsequently met under James's chairmanship, it was to consider which laws should be imposed on the new Gentile converts in Galatia and elsewhere—indeed wherever there were Gentile converts. It was a vital decision to differentiate Christianity from Judaism: a religion of grace from one of law (see John 1:17; Romans 3:20; Galatians 3:2,14). It was in this context that the Council had to consider which parts of the Law, if any, should be imposed on, or expected of, the Gentile converts.

Having firstly heard the views of the Christian Pharisees, the Council then heard from Peter who again said: "God, who knows the heart, showed that he accepted them by giving the Holy Spirit to them, just as he did to us. He made no distinction between us and them, for he purified their hearts by faith" (15:8,9). Peter summarizes his position with a resounding climax: "We believe it is through the grace of our Lord Jesus that we are saved, just as they are" (15:11). This speech by Peter is followed by Paul and Barnabas who tell of their mission among the Gentiles and how God confirmed their preaching and the inclusion of the Gentiles "with miraculous signs and wonders" (15:12). It was time to decide.

As a thorough and fair chairman, James listens to both sides of the argument and sums up what they have heard, in particular the evidence of Peter, who is regarded as the leading apostle. James confirms with a passage from Amos that it was always God's plan to include the Gentiles in salvation (15:15–18; Amos 9:11,12). Having affirmed this, he comes up with the simple and compelling conviction that "we should not make it difficult for the Gentiles who are turning to God" (15:19). Instead, the Council expects a minimum requirement from the Jewish Law, which falls into two parts in relation to food and one in relation to sex. In the matter of food, the Gentiles are not to eat meat which has been offered to idols, nor food from animals that have died from strangulation rather than having the blood drained through butchery. The law in relation to sex concerns abstinence from immorality (*porneías*) or fornication, which presumably means abstinence from any sex outside of marriage. Of these three laws, the food laws would not amount to a permanent prohibition but were a concession to Jewish sensibilities. Paul himself wrote a lengthy digression on food in 1 Corinthians 8 and Romans 14, declaring "all food clean", just as Jesus had implied earlier in Mark's Gospel (Romans 14:20; Mark 7:19b).

Having made this judgement, which had an element of compromise about it, James then makes sure it is properly communicated. They agree to write out their conclusion and instruction and to communicate it both by letter and by messengers or word of mouth (15:20,24–29). It is agreed therefore to send Paul and Barnabas back to Antioch as messengers with this instruction from Jerusalem (15:22), and for them to be accompanied by two "prophets", Judas and Silas (15:22b,33), to further confirm the Council's decision. When they arrive at Antioch, the decision of the Council, together with the words of Paul, Barnabas, Judas and Silas, greatly encourage the church there (15:30–35).

The Council had done its work under the able chairmanship of James. They had dealt with a fundamental issue facing the church, and in particular the Gentile converts. The Council had heard both sets of arguments, from the Christian Pharisaic party (15:5) and from the leading apostles, Peter and Paul (15:10–12). Judgement had been given in line with the apostles' teaching about grace and an instruction had been given as to which parts of the Mosaic Law should be observed. This was then communicated in written form as well as by word of mouth. The church in Antioch was greatly relieved and encouraged by the result. What is more, James had been a very effective chairman in guiding the church forward at this critical juncture.

James was not only a good chairman, but also an effective and vivid teacher of the faith. It is generally thought that James is the author of the epistle bearing his name found towards the end of the New Testament. It is written firstly to a Jewish constituency and is addressed to the "twelve tribes scattered among the nations" (James 1:1). It has a practical bent and is written in vivid and arresting language with considerable use of metaphor— e.g., the tongue is like a forest fire which is set ablaze by a small spark (James 3:5b). James emphasizes that if faith is real, it must be proven in actions and works (2:20–24). True faith should eschew partiality (2:1–9) and should not exploit the poor (5:1–6). The letter underscores the need for true wisdom (3:17) and humility (4:4–6), and throughout the letter there is a note of faith being tested but vindicated through patience (1:4,12; 5:7–12), and sometimes rewarded through answered prayer (5:13–18).

In many ways, it is a letter which could well have been written by a pastor, someone used to guiding others into fruitful decisions. It would be profitable to explore the link between James's skills as a chairman and his practical teaching as a church leader. There is no doubt that for a church to function well it needs both good pastors as well as effective chairmen and chairwomen.

James the martyr

We would be wrong simply to characterize James as a dry stick of a chairman, which is often how chairmen of councils or committees are seen: a necessary but not a very charismatic role of limited consequence! Probably the truth is that a good chairman is hardly noticed, but a bad one creates confusion, dissension, and possibly mayhem. But to characterize James wrongly as a bureaucrat would be a travesty of the truth and an injustice. He was the Lord's brother. He therefore had significant and almost unique understanding of the background of his brother. He had gifts of wisdom of which he speaks in his letter (James 3:13–17). He was undoubtedly a good and judicious chairman, as we have seen, but more than that, he was ready and prepared to die for his faith. And indeed, he did just that.

According to Josephus, a reliable historian, James was brought before the Sanhedrin around AD 62 after the appointment of a new High Priest, Ananus, and at a time when Roman governors sought once again to eradicate the Jewish sect now called Christians.[11] James was then accused of not observing the Jewish Law and, like Stephen, was stoned to death. Furthermore, Eusebius, the fourth-century bishop and chronicler of the early church, although not always accurate, quotes the historian Hegesippus (a Jewish Christian living c.AD 110–170), in maintaining the tradition of James's martyrdom albeit with a rather more vivid description.[12]

James, as the brother of Jesus, the chairman of the Jerusalem Council, which included apostles among their number, as one who wrote an epistle to the Judean church full of vibrant and pithy teaching in the tradition of Jewish wisdom literature, and as an eventual martyr of the church around AD 62, must surely be one of the most significant co-stars in the Acts of the Apostles.

---

[11]   Dunn, *Beginning from Jerusalem*, p. 1090ff.; citing Josephus 20:107–203.

[12]   Dunn, *Beginning from Jerusalem*, pp. 1094–95.

The apprentices: Timothy, Silas and Titus

Acts 16:1–40; 17:1–4; 2 Timothy 1:1–14;
Titus 1:1–16; Galatians 2:1–5

In the UK, there is a popular TV programme called *The Apprentice*, in which a proven entrepreneur, Lord Alan Sugar, chooses an apprentice from amongst a group of young and aspiring business entrepreneurs. They are given a number of tests and are fired one by one until there remains a single successful candidate who receives the benefit of working with Lord Sugar on a business venture. In the style of much reality TV, one or more candidates are fired each session, which makes for popular viewing. But the show has also lodged the idea of "an apprentice" in the minds of TV viewers and evokes the whole apprenticeship experience. In much of the building profession, many trades are learnt through schemes of apprenticeship (brick laying, electrical work and plumbing, roofing, plastering, carpentry and decorating etc.). Without these people nothing could be built. Likewise, in church work, apprenticeships are a sure way of learning the skills of the ministry.

Just as Jesus chose 12 apprentices to be his disciples, not all of whom succeeded (e.g. Judas), so too Paul followed the same pattern of training and choosing apprentices who would be with him before going out to fulfil their vocation. Three apprentices mentioned in the Acts of the Apostles, and also spoken of in the epistles, are Timothy, Silas and Titus. It seems that from early on Paul was aware of the need to train future leaders and that this was best done if they accompanied him on mission, heard him teach, preach and lead, and had regular opportunities to discuss issues relating to mission and ministry with him in the same way the disciples were able to do with Jesus (see Mark 3:13–19; 4:34b; 6:6–13; 10:41–45). This method of training, of being apprenticed to a senior leader or minister, has been the way of training ministers in the church from the beginning until now. It has the purpose of preparing individuals to become pastors and teachers themselves.

Timothy (Acts 16:1–5)

The first of those to be "appointed" as an apprentice was Timothy (16:1–5). He appears at the start of the second missionary journey Paul undertook without Barnabas—a senior colleague with whom, as we have seen, Paul had an altercation over whether to take John Mark, given he had turned back on the first missionary journey (15:36–41). Paul had returned to Lystra, where he and Barnabas had been on their first missionary journey and where he met the young Timothy, perhaps only 18 years of age (14:8–20). It is probable that Paul had already met Timothy on his first missionary journey when Timothy, then 16, had started to follow Christ. Timothy had obviously made a good beginning as a Christian, for the brothers at both Lystra and neighbouring Iconium spoke well of him (16:2).

Timothy's family was typical of many and prepared him for his later ministry in cosmopolitan cities like Ephesus, where there was both a Gentile and large Jewish population. His mother was Jewish and his father Greek. In his second letter to Timothy, Paul recalls the origin of Timothy's faith. Paul notes in that letter the faith of both Timothy's grandmother, Lois, and of his mother, Eunice. Both were Jews who had come to regard Jesus as the Messiah, as Paul himself had done after the appearance of Jesus on the Damascus Road (Acts 9:1–19; 2 Timothy 1:3–7). Timothy therefore was familiar with the Jewish scriptures stretching back generations through the Jewish part of his family. This knowledge was now fulfilled by his trust in Jesus as the Messiah. Paul appreciated and commented upon Timothy's rich lineage of faith (2 Timothy 1:5). When Paul arrived in Lystra at the start of what would be the most ground-breaking of all his missionary journeys, he certainly needed new companions. He would enter Europe, go to cities like Philippi, Thessalonica, Athens and Corinth. It seems that he quickly gained two companions in Timothy and Silas (16:19), as well as others, such as Luke, who were at times members of his missionary group (Acts 16:11ff.).

However, before Paul left on this journey, he took the radical step of circumcising Timothy, not so he might gain salvation thereby (which would have been quite contradictory to the Council of Jerusalem), or because there was any obligation to be circumcised on the grounds of faith, but simply to make Timothy more acceptable to any Jews that might enquire (see 1 Corinthians 9:19–23). It must have been a painful and possibly embarrassing episode, but one Paul felt necessary in the interests of mission. For his part, Timothy was prepared to undergo it, however reluctantly, for the sake of this calling. And no doubt Paul was persuasive.

Timothy was to have a long and challenging career as a missionary and then as a pastor, and as a companion and apprentice of Paul. It is clear from Paul's more personal second letter to Timothy, who was by then the pastor of the church in Ephesus, that he was not an especially robust individual, either physically or emotionally (1 Timothy 5:23; 6:12). Paul frequently tells Timothy to be strong (2 Timothy 1:6,7; 2:1) and to stir up the gifts within him. He is told to stay focused (2 Timothy 2:2–7), not to be ashamed of either Paul or the gospel (2 Timothy1:8), and to guard the gospel (2 Timothy 1:14). The impression is of a young man who is a little intimidated by the calling he has been given and of the need to command people, confront some occasionally, and to guard the deposit of the gospel which has been given to him (1 Timothy 6:20). In other words, it was a big step for him to move from being a close companion of Paul, from observing his ministry and taking part under his guidance, to being responsible for leading a church of the complexity and size as the church in Ephesus. Nevertheless, Timothy, at whatever the cost, and however unsuited he may have felt himself, stuck to the calling he had been given and turned his apprenticeship to good advantage. We do not know how it ended up for Timothy, but we do know that the church in Ephesus continued to thrive, although by the time of the letters to the churches in Revelation (c.AD 90), the church at Ephesus was commended for its orthodoxy but criticized for its lack of ardour (Revelation 2:1–7).

Silas (Acts 15:22–35; 16:1–40; 17:1–15; 18:1–6)

Silas and Timothy were the two new recruits and companions of Paul on his second missionary journey after he split with Barnabas and John Mark (15:36–41). As we have seen, Timothy appears the more sensitive character, while there seems to be no such side to Silas. He first emerged in Acts during the Council of Jerusalem. At the end of the Council, two people were sought from the Jerusalem church to go with Paul and Barnabas to convey the decision to the church in Antioch (15:22). The two were Silas and Judas Barsabbas. They were leaders in Jerusalem and later called prophets (15:32) and were to confirm the message in the Council's letter. If Silas already held this position in the Jerusalem church, it is probable that he was older than Timothy and more experienced in ministry. Having worked with Silas in conveying the Council of Jerusalem's decision to Antioch, Paul must have liked what he saw and asked Silas to accompany himself and Timothy (and it seems Luke) on his second missionary journey.

Paul's second missionary journey broke new ground. Initially they revisited the towns that Paul had visited on his first journey, where Paul delivered the decision of the Council (16:4). The churches were greatly strengthened by the news of the judgement, as well as by the ministry of Paul and his team (16:5).

Having completed this phase of their work, the mission faced something of an impasse until Paul, waiting at the port of Troas near the ancient city of Troy, received a vision in which a Macedonian "begs" him to come over to Macedonia and share the good news and help them (16:9–10). So, Paul, Timothy and Silas leave Asia for Europe and the Greek cities of that area.

In both Philippi and Thessalonica, Silas will see the personal cost as well as the excitement of ministry. It appears that Paul and Silas were working closely together in Philippi. Already, they had seen the conversion of Lydia and had been welcomed into her household. But soon after Paul was provoked by an evil spirit crying out from a fortune teller who repeatedly identified them as "servants of the Most High God who are telling you the way to be saved" (16:17). Although correct in what she (or the spirit within) was saying, her presence was a distraction and her words, although true, were a confusion to those hearing her, given the source of her inspiration. Paul exorcised her, but her master lost an ample income stream (for she was a slave girl) and was incensed (16:16b). Hauled before the magistrates by an angry owner on a less-than-certain charge, Paul and Silas were imprisoned until an earthquake precipitated their release and resulted in the conversion of the flabbergasted gaoler and his family (16:27–34). For Silas, it was a never-to-be-forgotten episode: singing hymns at midnight with Paul, released from gaol by earthquake, witnessing the conversion of their captor, and the apology of the magistrates when they discovered both were Roman citizens (16:35–40). Silas must have realized that there would not be a dull moment on mission with Paul, and that the church was being built by an extraordinary combination of circumstance and people.

From Philippi, they made their way to the principal regional city of Thessalonica lying on the Thermaic Gulf. There was a sizeable Jewish community there, and Paul, as usual, first went to preach to them, making known that Jesus was the Messiah and that in him all the promises and hopes of the Old Testament were fulfilled (17:2–4; as likewise in 13:32,33). The preaching was met with warm acceptance by some Jews, a large number of God-fearing Greeks, "and quite a few prominent women" (17:4), but also with distinct hostility bordering on violence. Again, Silas would have seen that the preaching of the good news, together with signs of the kingdom, produced a divided, but nonetheless fruitful response. The church to which they would address letters in the coming months and years would be one of the most fruitful (see 1 Thessalonians 1:2–10). The church became "a model to all the believers in Macedonia and Achaia". Once again Silas learnt the power of preaching, of example, and of the works of the Spirit, even in a context of great hostility. After all, their mission in the city lasted only three weeks (17:2) but was to great effect. Because of the disturbances, Paul and Silas had to leave for Berea under cover of darkness where Silas and Timothy lingered while Paul went on to Athens. Although Paul waited for Silas and Timothy in Athens, it seems that they were eventually reunited in Corinth for a still different type of mission. There was a big response there, and with a growing team Paul stayed on for a year and a half, having had another night vision (18:9–11).

Titus

Although there is no direct mention of Titus in Acts, it seems that the church in Corinth knew him well as an associate of Paul and knew that he had accompanied Paul to Jerusalem after the first missionary journey (see Galatians 2:1–5). However, although a Greek, Titus had been requested to be circumcised by either the Council of Jerusalem or Paul. He soon became a close companion of Paul's upon whom he came to depend (see 2 Corinthians 7:6,7,13–15) and whose presence was a great encouragement (see 2 Corinthians 2:13). Later, it was Titus who conveyed a letter from Paul to Corinth, and quite possibly the Epistle of 2 Corinthians itself (2 Corinthians 8:16–24). Titus appears as a warm-hearted, robust and resourceful individual with the responsibility of conveying Paul's messages to the churches and collecting money for the relief of the Judean Christians who were suffering hardship. He needed to be resourceful and confident to do this.

At some point, perhaps because he came from the island, Titus was appointed the pastor of the church in

Crete by Paul, who had travelled there quite possibly after his first trial in Rome. Paul wrote him a robust letter in which, quoting the Greek poet Epimenides, he infers Cretans are lazy, liars and gluttons (see Titus 1:12). It is a letter full of instructions, but which nevertheless has a beautiful summary of the gospel (3:3–8) in the midst of much forthright advice.

These three were the principal apprentices of Paul: Timothy the sensitive and more retiring pastor; Silas, who appears in the thick of it in the second missionary journey but then vanishes from the narrative; and Titus, the faithful co-worker of Paul on whom he depends but who is given the tough job of bringing the Cretan church into line and where he is remembered fondly to this day. Each contributed greatly to the life and mission of the early church.

To apprentice a future church leader remains a noble aim. From these three sketches we can see that apprentices can greatly vary in character and gifting, but the main aim in training them is to enable them to offer their whole selves in the service of Christ and to use their varied gifts to build up the church and extend God's mission to the world.

CHAPTER 9

The businesswoman: Lydia

Acts 16:6–40

The first stop of real significance in Paul's missionary journey into Europe was at Philippi in Macedonia. He had been summoned in a vision in the night by a Macedonian who asked him to "come over (the Aegean into Europe) and help us" (16:9). After sailing from Troas near the ancient city of Troy, via the island of Samothrace and the port of Neapolis, the party arrived at Philippi, the principal city of Macedonia. It was near here that the final battle between the forces of Mark Antony and Octavian (later Augustus), and those who had assassinated Julius Caesar, namely Brutus and Cassius, had taken place in 42 BC, some hundred years and more before Paul's arrival. Octavian would go on to defeat Mark Antony and Cleopatra and establish the Pax Romana from 27 BC till AD 14. Philippi was therefore a historic city, and, as the first city in Europe to receive the gospel, it was equally important. Moreover, one of the first people to believe in that city was Lydia, a businesswoman and a seller of purple goods.

Lydia was a remarkable businesswoman and entrepreneur accustomed to taking the initiative. She was someone who knew her own mind, was genuinely interested in knowing the truth and was already a seeker after God. She dealt in the highly prized purple dye and in purple goods, presumably clothing and textiles at the high-end of the retail market. She came from Thyatira on the Aegean, which is identified as the location of one of the seven churches of Asia Minor in the book of Revelation (2:18ff.). Dealing in purple dye probably required a special licence, for in the Roman Empire purple was the colour of the ruling class. Emperors and their families dressed in it. Indeed, in the eastern, later Byzantine empire, the phrase *porphyrogenetos* meant being "born into the purple", namely being a member of the royal family. Later, from Constantine onwards, purple would be worn by the ruling class and by bishops. In any event trade in purple dye was regulated. The dye itself came from a secretion of rock sea snails, the collection of which was controlled by the emperor. Lydia was therefore dealing with a much-prized commodity in what must have been a lucrative, élite-focused business.

For all her business acumen, her life did not entirely revolve around her work. Clearly, she was also on a spiritual quest. Lydia, we are told, was both a God-fearer and a person of prayer, whatever that would have meant to her. Although she lived in a pagan world in which multiple gods of various descriptions influenced most aspects of life, and in which there were many local cults, Lydia preferred to go to a quiet place outside the city for prayer. Luke tells us that she was a worshipper of God (*sebómenos*). As such she was one of a community of people thus called in Acts, including those like Cornelius the centurion. She probably knew of the Jewish community in Thyatira, her hometown, and if there was one in Philippi, she would have known of it, although we do not hear of Paul visiting a synagogue there.

Paul and his companions went to this place of prayer outside the city, fully expecting to find those who were on some kind of spiritual quest, and thus ready to listen. They found Lydia. She was curious about these strangers from Antioch and about what motivated them. They weren't like ordinary Jews: indeed, some of them, like Silas, Timothy and Luke, were Greek in origin and were accepted in this new Christian community without needing to become Jewish. They had travelled many miles to be there and were set on sharing their story and their "good news" about Jesus with the women there (16:13b). For men to be speaking to women in a public place may well have been novel and intriguing to Lydia. She listened with rapt attention, and more than that, as she did so, "the Lord opened her heart to respond to [the] message" (16:14). In this verse lies a mystery, which was that, as the message was announced and explained, God called: indeed, God opened her heart to his voice. Why that was not the case for the other women who were also listening to Paul is a further mystery, but perhaps they were not yet ready to open their hearts and receive the grace of God.

As a businesswoman accustomed to closing a deal, Lydia asked to be baptized straightaway. Like the Ethiopian eunuch, also a man used to making decisions, Lydia wanted to act at once. There was something contagious in their faith and she wanted to become a follower of Christ as they were. She also wanted to be baptized, presumably in the water of the river nearby, which marked out this place of prayer. So, Lydia and other members of her household, following her lead, were also baptized, after a clear explanation, one imagines, about what they were doing. Paul must have conducted her baptism, although he rarely did so (1 Corinthians 1:14–16). In keeping with her character, Lydia immediately invited Paul and his companions to a celebration in her roomy villa. Paul appears to have been a little reluctant initially, but Lydia was insistent: "If you consider me a believer in the Lord . . . come and stay at my house" (Acts 16:15b). Linking her invitation to their acceptance that she was now a Christian made it a critical matter. To turn her down was to risk at best a misunderstanding and at worst doubt over her profession of faith. That could jeopardize the founding of the church in Philippi. So, Paul, although perhaps reluctant at first, accepted the invitation and the church in Philippi was formed.

By the time Paul left, Philippi had become a church of great diversity, and one that was to become almost exemplary among the early churches. We know from the account in Acts that amongst others, the church comprised Lydia the businesswoman and her household, the gaoler of the city and his family, the slave girl who had been delivered from the spirit of divination, and possibly several other women who had listened to Paul by the river outside the city (16:13b). The church clearly grew further and became a powerful force in the region (2 Corinthians 8:1–4). It is also clear that the church in Philippi had a special place in Paul's heart. Writing some years later from prison in Rome in AD 60 (or, as some scholars think, from Ephesus in AD 55), he recalls their fellowship. He writes of the partnership in the gospel that he had with them from their first meeting (Philippians 1:5) and how he has them still "in his heart" (Philippians 1:7). He no doubt recalled both the suffering (a severe beating and imprisonment) and the moments of great joy as well. Encouraging them to have the same mind among themselves as Christ Jesus himself had in giving up the glory of heaven for human life, death and resurrection (Philippians 2:1–11), he calls on them to rejoice in the Lord always (Philippians 4:4), and to think about things that are positive, good and upbuilding (Philippians 4:8–9). The epistle remains much-loved for its glad note of joy and confidence in the way of Christ and may have been inspired in part by memories of his fruitful, if painful, visit there. It is not fanciful to think that he thought back to Lydia herself, the first convert recorded in Europe, and maybe imagined her reading his epistle aloud at a church meeting in her roomy house.

CHAPTER 10

The model couple: Priscilla and Aquila

Acts 18:1–28; Romans 16:3

In these next two chapters we come across three people or, to be precise, a married couple and a single man, whose lives were intertwined: Priscilla and Aquila, and Apollos. In this chapter, we look at the contribution of Aquila and Priscilla to the mission of the church in its early days, especially in Rome, Corinth and Ephesus.

Paul's first visit to Corinth was around AD 51–52. He arrived in Corinth from Athens, most likely by boat. It was not a long journey, but his arrival was marked by his own sense of vulnerability and weakness. As Paul said, "I came to you in weakness and fear, and with much trembling. My message and my preaching were not with wise and persuasive words, but with a demonstration of the Spirit's power, so that your faith might not rest on human wisdom, but on God's power" (1 Corinthians 2:3–5). At the heart of this message and preaching is the cross and the wisdom of God it demonstrates (see 1

Corinthians 1:18–25; 2:6–16). Paul may have felt weak, as he was conscious of being compared with the superlative rhetoricians who seemed to abound in Corinth, and who formed a point of contrast with Paul's unvarnished yet powerful style (see 2 Corinthians 11:5ff.).

Paul would stay in Corinth for about 18 months and was encouraged to do so by a vision in which the Lord addressed him as follows: "Do not be afraid; keep on speaking, do not be silent. For I am with you, and no-one is going to attack and harm you, because I have many people in this city" (Acts 18:9,10). So, Paul stayed on, teaching the word of God. A more human reason for staying on at Corinth, in what was a more settled existence for Paul, was the presence of Aquila and Priscilla, and a little later the arrival from Macedonia of his colleagues, Silas and Timothy (18:5). Aquila and Priscilla were to become important companions of Paul, and crop up frequently in his correspondence and Acts.

Priscilla and Aquila

When Paul arrived in Corinth from Athens, he soon heard of this Christian couple called Aquila and Priscilla. They had lately come from Rome as all the Jews had been expelled from the capital by Emperor Claudius (AD 41–54) in AD 49 because of riots in the city around the person of "Chrestus" (Christ). This event is recorded by the Roman historian Suetonius in his life of Claudius.[13] Aquila and Priscilla had also had time to establish themselves as businesspeople over the previous two years in the city. Like Paul they were tentmakers and Paul quickly found work with them, so as not to burden anyone with his upkeep. Furthermore, Paul seems to have lived in their apartment (18:3), and quite possibly the quickly growing church in Corinth first met in their house or apartment, before moving to the home of Titius Justus (18:7).

What is clear is that Aquila and Priscilla were already Christians when they arrived in Corinth. They probably became Christians in Rome through the movement of Christians there in the early years of the church (c.AD 45–49). They were a mature, resourceful and well-equipped couple, likely to have an impact wherever they went, and would quickly form part of the leadership team of the church in Corinth, especially with the arrival from Macedonia of Silas and Timothy (18:5a). One might imagine that over the next 18 months they led the rapidly growing church in Corinth together with Paul, gaining in the process much useful insight into leading a church. Initially, Paul preached openly in the synagogue. The synagogue leader Crispus (18:8) believed and was dramatically and personally baptized by Paul (1 Corinthians 1:14). But when Paul faced intense opposition, which led to a court case before

---

[13]   Suetonius, *The Twelve Caesars: The Life of Divus Claudius* §25, tr. Robert Graves (Harmondsworth: Penguin, 2007), p. 195.

the Proconsul Gallio (Proconsul of Achaea, AD 50–51), the son of Seneca the Elder from Cordoba, Spain, Paul left off preaching in the synagogue and the church met instead in the homes of Aquila and Priscilla and Titius Justus. Gallio dismissed the case against Paul, having judged that differences over Jewish theology were of no concern to Roman courts (18:14–17), although with the increase of emperor worship all this was to change.

The result of Gallio's decision was that the new synagogue ruler, Sosthenes, who had succeeded the converted Crispus, was beaten up by his own people from the synagogue. They were frustrated at the way events had turned against them. At this point Paul also decided it was time to leave, but so impressed had he been with Aquila and Priscilla that he took them with him, and presumably Silas and Timothy also, and together they sailed to Syria, putting in at Ephesus *en route.*

Ministry in Ephesus

So, after 18 months, Paul left Corinth following a very productive mission which had founded an important church, but one that would be trouble in the years ahead. So important had Aquila and Priscilla been in supporting him, in hosting the church, and acting as pastors and teachers, that they had become invaluable to Paul. And since Paul would be breaking new ground in the important city of Ephesus (twice the size of

Corinth), he took them with him.

We also notice that in telling the story, Luke reverses the names of the couple twice (18:18,19). Whereas at the beginning of the chapter the couple are introduced to the narrative as Aquila and Priscilla, now Luke, and later Paul (see Romans 16:3), refer to them as Priscilla and Aquila. This perhaps was because Priscilla was the more spiritually gifted and outgoing of the two. This may be wide of the mark, but we can envisage Aquila as the conscientious businessman and tentmaker, able to run a business, and Priscilla as the gregarious and challenging wife and budding deaconess who would both nurture, and challenge and correct. This is not an unusual combination in a married couple. Sometimes such a pair are characterized as "the hedgehog and the rhino"!

Paul sailed across the Aegean to Ephesus near modern-day Selçuk, inland from Kuşadası. Paul did not intend to stay long there. He wanted to get to Jerusalem for a festival, but he promised he would return as soon as possible.[14] Paul then made haste for Jerusalem after having a haircut because of a vow he had made, and after making a brief appearance at the synagogue in Ephesus (18:19) where he may have been able to persuade a number of Jews. He left Ephesus promising to return, and it seems he appointed Priscilla and Aquila to oversee any ongoing work there. Timothy and Silas are not mentioned.

---

[14] Wright, *Paul: A Biography*, pp. 229ff.

Before Paul returned to Ephesus several months later (19:1–41), Priscilla and Aquila had taken up the role of encouraging the infant church. It appears there was a Christian congregation in the city, formed from visiting Christians and possibly from some enquirers following Paul's initial synagogue visit (18:19b). At any rate, there was enough of a community for a visitor called Apollos to come and speak there and for Priscilla and Aquila to attend. Apollos was an impressive speaker from Alexandria, an intellectual and spiritual centre in the eastern Mediterranean. He had received some instruction in the Christian life but was nonetheless lacking in some respects. Luke tells us that Apollos was "a learned man with a thorough knowledge of the Scriptures" (18:24). Not only that, but his style was arresting: "He had been instructed in the way of the Lord, and spoke with great fervour and taught about Jesus accurately, though he knew only the Baptism of John" (18:25). In other words, he was good in so far as he went, but his understanding was deficient.

Others might have been somewhat in awe of Apollos, either because of his learning and background—the sophisticated circles of Alexandria—or because of the fervour of his delivery, but not so Priscilla and Aquila. One suspects that it was Priscilla who was the more forthright of the pair, the one ready to correct who sought to complete Apollos's understanding of the faith for the future benefit of the church. It seems there were a number (Luke says 12) in Ephesus whose understanding went up to but not beyond John the Baptist's witness to Jesus (see Acts 19:1–7). This means that they recognized Jesus as the Messiah and John's role as his forerunner. It means that they participated in the baptism of repentance for the forgiveness of sins, yet knew nothing about the assurance of forgiveness through the cross, and the gift of the Holy Spirit to seal, empower and sanctify the believer. Indeed, Apollos resembled these Ephesian elders, presumably a group of church leaders in a "church community" in Ephesus whose understanding of the Christian faith was partial, for they had neither received the Spirit nor been baptized in the name of Jesus for the forgiveness of sins. Paul would make sure that these Ephesian elders were introduced to full-blown Christianity: belief in Jesus, his gift of forgiveness, and the reception of the Holy Spirit (19:1–7).

What Paul was to do for the Ephesian elders, Priscilla and Aquila did for Apollos. They invited him back to their home from the synagogue (18:26). In the privacy of that environment, with no possibility of Apollos losing face publicly, they explained "the way of God more adequately" (18:26). There is no doubt that Apollos's eyes were opened and he may have received the Spirit for the first time through their prayers, although this is not explicitly stated.

Thus Priscilla and Aquila, who formed a remarkable combination, had an invaluable behind-the-scenes and up-front ministry for the church. The importance of such a ministry cannot be overemphasized. The limelight is often not the best place to highlight a necessary step to be taken. But with great wisdom, perception and human understanding, they completed in Apollos what had been begun but was as yet unfinished (Philippians 1:6 for this principle).

At some point in the next four years, Priscilla and Aquila returned to Rome. We find Paul greeting Priscilla and Aquila in the final chapter of his great Epistle to the Romans (16:3). It is thought that Paul wrote that epistle in AD 57, quite possibly in Corinth. Paul's ministry in Ephesus can be dated from AD 53–56, during which time he may have travelled back to Corinth in c.AD 53 or 54, for what has been called the "painful visit", before returning to Ephesus where he may have been imprisoned, and returning to Corinth later in AD 56.[15] Whatever Paul's precise movements in this period, we can be in no doubt of his estimation of Priscilla and Aquila. He puts them in pole position in his lengthy greetings to the Roman church (see Romans 16:1–27). And he pays them the honour of telling everyone that they risked their lives for him and that the Gentile churches owe them a deep debt of gratitude. And once again, as in Corinth and no doubt in Ephesus, the church met in their home and benefited from their combined wisdom, enthusiasm and leadership. What a couple!

---

[15]   See Wright, *Paul: A Biography*, p. 434.

CHAPTER 11

The eloquent speaker: Apollos

Acts 18:24–28; 1 Corinthians 3:1–23

Although we have already touched on the life and ministry of Apollos of Alexandria, there is more to learn from him and about him. He was a first-century Alexandrian Jew. The city of Alexandria was founded by Alexander the Great in 331 BC and was to become the great intellectual hub of the eastern Mediterranean and an important centre of Jewish studies. It was here, soon after the city was founded, that the Septuagint, the Greek translation of the Jewish Scriptures was made, *c.*285–247 BC, by 72 Jewish scholars—six, it is said, from each tribe of Israel. This was in the reign of Ptolemy II, one of the Pharaohs of later Egypt in succession to Ptolemy, one of Alexander's generals. It was also in Alexandria that Philo (*c.*20 BC—AD 50) explored the links between the Jewish Scriptures and Greek philosophy. Latterly, the city became known for its soaring lighthouse, splendid library and invasions, first by Caesar and then by Octavian (Augustus) in pursuit of Antony and Cleopatra (30 BC). It is thus a city rich in Greek, Roman and Jewish history. It would become one of the great Christian cities of the ancient world, boasting the Gospel writer Mark as the founder of the Egyptian (Coptic) church. At some point before AD 52, when Paul first arrived in Ephesus, Apollos—named after the pagan messenger of the gods—became part of the Jewish community in Alexandria which followed the teaching of John the Baptist. As a prophet of Israel, John the Baptist (Luke 7:18–35), had secured a wide following in the Levant, not all of whom had yet become Christians (i.e. baptized followers of Christ).

When Apollos arrived in Ephesus at the same time as Paul, Priscilla and Aquila, we are told that he had recently come from Alexandria (Acts 18:24). Furthermore, he was learned—having a natural disposition to be well informed—and had a thorough knowledge of the Old Testament (18:24). More than that, he had begun to follow the teaching of John the Baptist and what might be called the early Galilean teaching of Jesus.[16] This instruction might well have come from the large Jewish community of Alexandria, some of whom were as yet imperfect followers of Jesus. After all, some Jews from Egypt were present in Jerusalem on the Day of Pentecost and heard the apostles speaking, quite possibly in their own language of Coptic (2:10). As we have seen, what Apollos may have lacked in knowledge, he certainly

---

[16]   Dunn, *Beginning from Jerusalem*, p. 757.

made up for in conviction, as he spoke in the synagogue about Jesus with "great fervour" (18:25). But, as Luke says, "he knew only the baptism of John" (18:25b). It was then that Priscilla and Aquila with great tact and skill filled in the missing parts of Apollos's teaching and testimony and brought him to a full knowledge of Jesus and the truth.

What appears to have been lacking in Apollos's faith was the knowledge of Christ's redemptive action through his crucifixion and resurrection: the forgiveness of sin, victory over death, but also the gift of the Spirit. Just as the Ephesian elders of 19:1–7 had to be challenged by Paul about whether they had received the Spirit, and then did so, likewise Apollos most probably received the Spirit through the ministry of Aquila and Priscilla. "In both cases it was the presence or absence of the Spirit which was decisive; the assessment of Priscilla and Aquila on the issue was as Paul's. For Luke, once more it is the coming of the Spirit which is the central and most crucial factor in conversion-initiation and in Christian identity."[17]

Apollos therefore represents a group of people who were more than God-fearers, who knew something of the ministry of Christ at its outset, but not all of it. They were seeking to follow him in the absence of full knowledge and understanding, but nevertheless had real fervour and conviction. Apollos was such a person, and he must have been representative of a wider group

---

[17]   Dunn, *Beginning from Jerusalem*, p. 759.

of people who knew in part, but whose knowledge and faith was partial. How best to complete what had begun in them would be a matter for careful consideration and sensitive encouragement.

Apollos in Corinth

While Apollos's faith was completed in Ephesus with the help of Priscilla and Aquila, the place where his gifts were especially deployed was in the province of Achaia, and in Corinth.

After the completion of his conversion in Ephesus, Apollos went to Corinth, from where Priscilla and Aquila had recently come. He was encouraged to go there by the "brothers and sisters" in Ephesus, was warmly welcomed, and then set about preaching in the synagogue, "proving from the Scriptures that Jesus was the Christ" (18:28) and was a great help to those "who by grace had believed" (18:27b).

It appears that Apollos was a very eloquent and compelling speaker, and from Paul's letter to the Corinthians we gather that he soon had a strong following in the church (see 1 Corinthians 1:12). This was more a commentary on the impressionable nature of the Corinthian church than a desire of Apollos to build up a personal following there. Nevertheless, the Corinthian church—with its superficial estimation of speakers, often looking for rhetorical style rather than substance—had divided its allegiance around different personalities (see 1 Corinthians 3:1–9). Their immaturity, which made them prize style over content and rhetoric over wisdom, gave Paul an opportunity to make a profound reflection on the subject of true wisdom and unity in the opening chapters of 1 Corinthians. He recalls that when he first arrived at Corinth, he did not come "with eloquence or superior wisdom as I proclaimed to you the testimony about God" (1 Corinthians 2:1). Rather, determining to know nothing except "Jesus Christ and him crucified" (1 Corinthians 2:2), "I came to you in weakness and fear, and with much trembling. My message and my preaching were not with wise and persuasive words, but with a demonstration of the Spirit's power, so that your faith might not rest on human wisdom, but on God's power" (1 Corinthians 1:3–5). Paul goes on to speak of the type of wisdom found in his preaching: a secret wisdom, hidden in the ages (1 Corinthians 2:7); a God-given wisdom which seemed like foolishness as demonstrated in the cross but which was, nevertheless, the means of salvation (1 Corinthians 1:25); and finally, a Spirit-inspired wisdom (1 Corinthians 2:10b–16).

Paul wrote in this way about the wisdom of God displayed through his preaching, which centred on the cross but was conveyed not with plausible words of wisdom but in weakness and trembling, because faith must not rest on the polish or intellectual capacity or erudition of the speaker, but on the true spiritual reality of the content of the message. Although Apollos had by this point been fully briefed by Priscilla and Aquila on the true Christian message centred on Jesus and the crucifixion and resurrection, the very eloquence with which he spoke was a snare for the Corinthians. For they were tempted, through no fault of Apollos, to base their faith more on the stellar qualities of his style than on the spiritual truth of what he said. In this way, groupings emerged in the Corinthian church, in which some said they were "of Paul", others "of Apollos", and others of some superlative apostles (i.e., messengers) as indicated by Paul later in the correspondence (see 2 Corinthians 10 and 11). What exactly Apollos said about this tendency in the Corinthian church we do not know, but we would like to think that, along with Paul, he would seek to dampen down any incipient following of himself rather than Christ. For Paul makes clear that each of them—Paul, Peter and Apollos—are merely God's instruments and gifts to them, and that all have their origins in God's grace and gifting entirely. As Augustine of Hippo wrote, "what have you received that is not a gift from God?" Because of this there was to be no more boasting, only a recognition that all came from God.

We hear little more about Apollos, but he represents a polished, erudite speaker with a compelling style who is both orthodox and attractive. As such he was an asset to the church, but also a temptation. The temptation was to be taken up with his obvious ability and fail to attend to the content of his message. In an immature church, as in Corinth, prone to look only on the surface and not beneath, this constituted a danger and one that needed to be pointed out. Jerome, the translator of the Vulgate (Latin Bible), maintained that Apollos spent some time in Crete, disillusioned with Corinth before returning there as an elder. Later scholars, such as Luther, thought that Apollos could have been the author of the Epistle to the Hebrews, but there is no conclusive proof of this. He does remain one of the notable advocates of the Christian faith in its early years, however: humble enough to be corrected by Priscilla and Aquila and persuasive enough to leave a lasting mark on the early church.

The author: Luke

Acts 1:1–11; 16:5–15; 20:7—21:26;
27:1—28:16 (notice the "we")

Our final co-star of the Acts of the Apostles is the author himself, Luke. Without his careful record, we would have no knowledge of the beginnings of the post-Pentecost church and its spread through the Near East and Europe. Indeed, without his narrative, there would be a gaping hole in our understanding of the early church, its beginning at Pentecost, its *modus operandi* in the early years, and the scope of its mission as well as its main leaders and opponents.

Luke is thought to have been a Gentile doctor, most probably from Antioch, a polished writer and historian and a companion of Paul. He wrote a two-volume work made up of his Gospel and the Acts of the Apostles, which together give us both a vivid account of the life of Christ and the beginnings of the early church, from the ascension of Jesus and the gift of the Spirit at

Pentecost onwards. Luke's work, no doubt moved and created by the Spirit through his own desire to record it, is therefore of inestimable value. Can anyone imagine the New Testament without it?

It seems that during Paul's time at Antioch, where he was taken by Barnabas in *c.*AD 46, he met Luke. The latter had become a Christian and had joined the Antioch church with its mixed congregation of Jew and Gentile and strong missionary outlook. Soon after that, Luke became a companion of Paul, travelling with him (see the passages above containing the pronoun "we") on his second missionary journey and on his final voyage to Rome after Paul had appealed to be tried by Caesar (Acts 25:10,11). Paul records Luke's presence with him in three places in his writings in AD 55/56. When writing to the Colossians, Paul writes: "Our dear friend Luke, the doctor, and Demas send greetings" (Colossians 4:14) and again in later correspondence from Rome to Philemon and Timothy (Philemon 1:24 and 2 Timothy 4:11). It is clear from this that Luke was a close and loyal companion of Paul.

We cannot be exact in our dating of Luke's Gospel or the Acts of the Apostles, but it is quite possible that some time elapsed between the two Lucan books which were presented separately to Theophilus (Luke 1:3 and Acts 1:1). The most likely date for the Gospel and Acts is around the mid-70s, after Peter and Paul's execution and the conclusion of the Jewish War (AD 66–70), with the fall of Jerusalem to the armies of Titus in AD 70.

This would have given Luke time to collect the material for his Gospel from different sources. Mark's Gospel, already written, served as a common source for Luke and Matthew. A further source called Q (*Quelle,* the German word for source) and common to the synoptic Gospels, scholars (e.g. Kloppenborg) believe contained collected sapiential (wisdom) sayings of Jesus from the mid first century AD. In addition, there were Luke's own sources, especially Mary's account of the nativity either in oral or written form.

Luke needed time to assemble the material that he would use in the book of Acts in his careful and theological narrative of the church's early ministry.

As we look at Acts as a whole, we can observe a number of themes close to Luke's heart. Undoubtedly, he recognized the work of the Spirit as the presence of Jesus in the church, empowering it for mission even when faced with opposition (4:13–22). Indeed, as the Spirit came upon the infant church it received power to witness (1:8). Not only that, but the Spirit gifted the church for its role in the world (2:17,18). As we have highlighted the co-stars in the Acts of the Apostles, we have seen the range of this gifting: gifts of encouragement and discernment (Barnabas); gifts of evangelism (Philip); gifts of witness and martyrdom (Stephen); gifts of leadership (Cornelius); gifts of chairmanship and wisdom (James); gifts of hospitality and welcome (Lydia); gifts of encouragement and teaching (Priscilla and Aquila); gifts of prophecy (Agabus); gifts of speaking (Apollos); and a gift of writing (Luke). All these gifts which built up the church and enabled its mission were inspired by the Spirit, who activates and inspires innate human talent.

The church was also a community which looked after the poor. In his Gospel, Luke especially highlights Jesus's care of the poor and the right stewardship of money (Luke 16; 19:1–10). And in Acts, Luke shows how this Spirit directs the Christian community to care for the needs of the poor (2:42–47; 4:32–37), and how Paul will also fulfil this responsibility by taking money from the Gentile churches to the impoverished Christians of Judea (Romans 15:25–28).

If Luke's narrative demonstrates the direction and empowering by the Spirit of the church in its mission of making Jesus known as Lord and Saviour (see Acts 2:29–36), he is also clear about the centrality of the message. It is about the Lordship of Christ, who confronts Paul on the road to Damascus (9:5; 10:42; 17:29–31), and whose message of forgiveness of sins through repentance and faith (2:38,39) should be preached to all people.

Luke presents a narrative centred around the two leading apostles, Peter and Paul, called and equipped by God and uniquely prepared to make known the gospel to the ancient world. Both will find their earthly end in Rome, the capital of the ancient world, and there their lives will be sacrificed in the cause of Christ. But their work depends on a whole group of co-stars: apprentices, prophets, fellow workers, leaders and householders, vital and integral to the apostles' work, and it is their contribution that this short book highlights. Equally, it is making our own contribution, according to our own gifts and calling, that enables the mission of God to go forward in the world today. Have you identified your own particular gifts and the contribution you can uniquely make to the mission of the church in today's world?

Bible Study Group Questions

Chapter 1: The encourager: Barnabas

Acts 4:36–37; 9:26–29; 11:25–30; 13:1–3; 15:36–41

1. Why was Joseph (Barnabas) given the nickname "Barnabas"? What nickname might be given to you? (If the group knows you sufficiently well, they can have a go and say why.)
2. What lay at the root of Barnabas's generosity?
3. What was it about Barnabas that made him the link between the newly converted Saul and the apostles in Jerusalem? (See Acts 9:26–30.) When might these gifts of personality be useful or vital in the church?
4. Why was Barnabas the perfect man to go down to Antioch? (See Acts 11:22–26.)
5. What made Barnabas go to Tarsus to find Saul (Paul)? What characteristics and gifts did he show in doing this? (See Acts 11:25,26.)
6. Why did Paul and Barnabas make such a good team? Are there any indications of this in their first missionary journey? (See Chapters 13–14.)

7. What was the cause of Paul and Barnabas's rift (see 15:36–41)? Were they both right? What does it teach us about Christian work?

Chapter 2: The first martyr: Stephen

Acts 6:5,8–15; 7:1—8:1

1. What was so special about Stephen?
2. Why was the Temple such a point of issue between Stephen and the Sanhedrin?
3. What did the Sanhedrin fear to lose?
4. What was the root cause of the dispute between Stephen and the Sanhedrin, and what were the emotions involved? Was the Temple redundant?
5. Why is Christianity so prone to persecution?
6. What effect did the stoning of Stephen have on the church?

Chapter 3: The evangelist: Philip

Acts 6:1–7; 8:1–40; 21:1–9

1. How would you describe the gift of an evangelist, and in what ways is an evangelist different from a witness?

2. Is it right to consider the blood of the martyrs the seed of the church? How did persecution act as a spur to mission in the early church?

3. What was remarkable about Philip's mission to Samaria?

4. Why was it necessary for the Samaritan converts to be prayed for to receive the Spirit by the apostles? Is church order important?

5. In what ways was Simon's heart not right before God? In what ways can money corrupt the ministry of the church?

6. In what ways did the Spirit orchestrate the evangelism of the Ethiopian official? What sort of a man was he?

7. How does the book of Isaiah reflect the gospel in its prophecies?

8. What characteristics particularly impress you in Philip?

Chapter 4: The go-between: Ananias

Acts 9:10–19

1. How do you envisage Ananias as a character?

2. Why is he so important in the story of Saul's conversion?

3. What would Ananias have thought and felt about God's request of him?

4. What was so impressive about Ananias's conduct when he arrived at Straight Street?
5. What difference did it make to Saul?
6. Have you ever had to change your mind about someone and treat them differently? How did it work out?
7. What have you learnt from this story?

Chapter 5: The God-fearing centurion: Cornelius

Acts 10:1–48

1. How much Spirit-led orchestration was required to bring the Gentiles into the gospel community? What prejudices or traditions had to be overcome?
2. What was so special about Cornelius?
3. How quick was Peter to grasp what was being asked of him?
4. What features of Peter's address in Cornelius's house especially strike you? Are there any particular ideas or phrases that stand out?
5. How does God himself take the initiative through the Spirit in this event, and why is that?
6. Did it come naturally to Peter to welcome in the Gentiles?
7. Have you had the experience of drawing boundaries to God's grace and finding that they

are not God's boundaries? Can you give any examples?

8. This was a shift in the tectonic plates of Judaism. Was it plain sailing ever afterwards? What else had to be addressed in the future? (See Galatians 2:11–21.)

9. How would you sum up the significance of this passage?

Chapter 6: The prophet: Agabus

Acts 11:19–30; 21:1–16

1. How does New Testament prophecy differ from that in the Old Testament?
2. Can we expect it in today's church?
3. What is the purpose of prophecy in the church?
4. What was the effect of Agabus's prophecies in Acts?
5. Have you come across the benefit of prophecy in church life? And the misuse of the gift?!
6. How do you know when you have the gift? Can you give an example of using this gift yourself?
7. Would Agabus have been understood in your church?

Chapter 7: The chairman: James

Acts 15:1–35; 21:17–26; Galatians
1:18–24; The Epistle of James

1. What would it have been like growing up in the family of Jesus?
2. How did James receive recognition in the early church in Judea?
3. What was the issue that needed to be resolved in the Council of Jerusalem?
4. What makes a good chairperson? What qualities can you discern in James's chairmanship? What happens if you have a bad chairperson?
5. What do you think of the resolution that was passed and the spirit in which it was formulated?
6. Can you see any connection between James's Epistle and his ability as a chairman?
7. Are Councils necessary in the life of the church? Could we do without them?

Chapter 8: The apprentices: Timothy, Silas and Titus

Acts 16:1–40; 17:1–4; 2 Timothy 1:1–14;
Titus 1:1–16; Galatians 2:1–5

1. How did Paul set about training his apprentices?
2. From what you know of these three, how varied in character were they?
3. What should be your main aim in training an apprentice?
4. Understanding, character and gifting are thought to be the three areas to nurture when training another for Christian work. Is that a fair summary of the task?
5. Have you ever trained another, or been trained for Christian work? How effective was it for you or them?
6. What else should we be aware of in training others?
7. How successful was Paul's training of Timothy, Silas and Titus?

Chapter 9: The businesswoman: Lydia

Acts 16:6–40

1. What kind of character do you think Lydia was?
2. What do you think had already happened in her heart, even before she met Paul? What do you think we can learn from that?
3. How do you understand "The Lord opened her heart" (16:14b)? What do we do in evangelism? What does God do?
4. Why was baptism important?
5. What type of ministry was Lydia going to have?
6. Why was Paul initially reluctant to go to her house? Why was it important to do so?
7. Why was Philippi a typical church? And why is the church at its best quite unlike any other community?
8. What else have you learnt from this story?

Chapter 10: The model couple: Priscilla and Aquila

Acts 18:1–28; Romans 16:3

1. How do you think Aquila and Priscilla became Christians?
2. Why were they such a valuable couple to Paul?

3. What do you think were their respective gifts and why?
4. How did they set about correcting Apollos?
5. What was good about the way they did it?
6. How did their ministry benefit the church?
7. Have you known couples like this and what was their impact?

Chapter 11: The eloquent speaker: Apollos

Acts 18:24–28; 1 Corinthians 3:1–23

1. In what ways was Apollos's faith lacking?
2. How did Priscilla and Aquila set about correcting or fulfilling him?
3. What were Apollos's strengths? How might they have been a snare to him?
4. What was Apollos's contribution in Corinth? What were the pitfalls in ministering in Corinth?
5. What are the strengths and weaknesses of eloquence?
6. What should be the right relationship of style and substance in Christian ministry?
7. How is God's wisdom different from ours?
8. What have you learnt from Apollos?

Chapter 12: The author: Luke

Acts 1:1–11; 16:5–15; 20:7—21:26;
27:1—28:16 (notice the "we")

1. What would the New Testament be like if we did not have the writings of Luke?
2. What made Luke write down his narrative of the early church?
3. Why is writing or scripture so important to the Christian faith?
4. What do you like especially about Luke's writings?
5. What does the personal experience of Luke (the "we" passages in Acts) add to the record?
6. Which "co-star" are you especially drawn to?
7. What do we learn about the mission of God and the church from these studies?

Select bibliography

Basil of Caesarea, *On the Holy Spirit*, tr. Stephen Hildebrand (Crestwood, NY: St Vladimir's Press, 2011).

Dunn, James D. G., *Beginning from Jerusalem, Vol II of Christianity in the Making* (Grand Rapids, MI: Wm. B. Eerdmans, 2009).

Jeremias, Joachim, *Jerusalem in the Time of Jesus: An Investigation into Economic and Social Conditions during the New Testament Period*, tr. M. E. Dahl (London: SCM Press, 1969).

Stott, John, *The Message of Acts* (Leicester: InterVarsity Press, 1991).

Suetonius, *The Twelve Caesars*, tr. Robert Graves (Harmondsworth: Penguin, 2007).

Whitworth, Patrick, *Gospel for the Outsider: The Gospel in Luke & Acts* (Durham: Sacristy Press, 2014).

Patrick Whitworth, *Gospel of Fulfilment: Exploring the Gospel of Matthew* (Durham: Sacristy Press, 2019).

Whitworth, Patrick, *Gospel of the Kingdom: Exploring the Gospel of Mark* (Durham: Sacristy Press, 2021).

Whitworth, Patrick, *Gospel of the Trinity: Exploring the Gospel of John* (Durham: Sacristy Press, 2023).

Wright, Tom, *Paul: A Biography* (London: SPCK, 2020).

EU GPSR Authorized Representative:

LOGOS EUROPE, 9 rue Nicolas Poussin, 17000 La Rochelle, France

contact@logoseurope.eu

www.ingramcontent.com/pod-product-compliance
Lightning Source LLC
Chambersburg PA
CBHW060956050726
47592CB00003B/1241